Against Architecture

Franco La Cecla

D1466665

Translated from the Italian
by Mairin O'Mahony

Against Architecture
Franco La Cecla. Translated by Mairin O'Mahony
© 2012 PM Press
All rights reserved. No part of this book may be transmitted by any means without
permission in writing from the publisher.

ISBN: 978–1–60486–406–9
Library of Congress Control Number: 2011927956

Cover art by Gent Sturgeon
Cover layout by John Yates / www.stealworks.com
Interior design by briandesign

10 9 8 7 6 5 4 3 2

PM Press
PO Box 23912
Oakland, CA 94623
www.pmpress.org

The Green Arcade
1680 Market Street
San Francisco, CA 94102–5949
www.thegreenarcade.com

Printed in the USA on recycled paper, by the Employee Owners of Thomson-Shore
in Dexter, Michigan.
www.thomsonshore.com

Contents

Acknowledgments

AS EVA SERRA, FRIEND AND THE SOUL OF BARCELONA
Regional, says, one writes books to find a way of making sense
of the years one has just lived through. In this case she is right,
because I needed to work out why one thing and another have
led me to become deeply involved and get into a knock-down
drag-out with architecture. Eva has to take some of the responsibility, as do Josep Acebillo and Emiliano Armani, who pains-
takingly led me through the new European and American
architecture and got me involved in the Piacenza experiment,
an attempt to construct a project "as if architects didn't exist."
With him in making my outlook less myopic are Sara Donati,
Stefano Savona, Piera Zanini, Silvia Bartolini, Azzurra della
Penna, Madelaine Fava, Sofia Lorefice, Katia Accossato, and
Lorenzo Romita.

To Renzo Piano for making me consider reality, to understand from within the fascination of a practice in which, apart
from my doubts about the entire discipline, he remains one of
the greatest masters. I owe him for the friendship and the awe
of finding myself joking with him as if we were kids.

To Kenneth Frampton I owe for a magnificent discussion
at New Year's in New York at Madelaine's house.

Francesca Gori and Unidea gave me the wherewithal to
deepen my approach to the theme of the story of suburbia in
Europe.

This is an argumentative book, and many people will
reproach me for getting in the middle of it all. I regret if people

take it personally. I still believe in the value of dialog on ideas and think it a blessing if it is lively and stimulating rather than tranquil and conciliatory, but I admit that it could be boring to find oneself involved in a debate without having been invited.

Introduction

THERE WAS A MOMENT, AND IT LASTED QUITE A WHILE, when Europe looked towards America as the font of inspiration for city planning and architecture that was not bogged down in tired repetitions of the nineteenth century. On one side there was America with a new and different concept of community living and of the symbolism given to this community togetherness; on the other side there was Europe looking towards the east, towards the socialist experimentations in housing quarters. America represented the capacity for modernization that was lacking in Europe, represented a model of society in which mobility and ethnic differences constituted a blending of new opportunities.

Today this dream seems to have disappeared. It is America that appears to be looking elsewhere, that seems to be looking for an urban life-in-common that is more European and an architectural model that is more "classic." If one wanders around New York—as I did with my architect friend Emiliano Armani, to whom I owe the viewpoint that I am trying to express here—one realizes that the symbolic excellence of American modernity has transformed itself into a turgid showcase, a shrine not for preserving the fabric of humanity and its sense of community, but a physical format that is by now merely a brand rather than an urban configuration.

The same thing is happening on the West Coast: America is closing itself up in an architectonic planning nostalgia that has much to do with the fears that traverse the nation. What constitutes these fears? Fear of terrorism, fear of the economic crisis, fear of the loss of supremacy, but most of all a generic fear, vague and indistinct, the fear of launching oneself into the creation of something new.

In such a situation it is practically impossible for projects, plans, and visions to present themselves forcefully as models of the new. If it was the American city that intrigued Salvador Dalí and Le Corbusier, if it was what inspired surrealism far more than the products of the European avant-garde, nowadays this impetus is at a complete standstill. In the meantime all the tired old formalistic and meaningless models—of towers, skyscrapers, and skylines—are pervading the world of the Asian Tiger, of the new-rich Latin Americas and the oil-rich Arab powers, and are shooting up where they are the obligatory symbol of economic growth: in Dubai, Songdo, Shanghai, Hanoi, Istanbul, Mumbai, and Astana. And the average cities of China, India, and Latin America are obsessively following the housing models concocted by the socialist countries and later in the French suburbs of the 1930s on.

It's as if the rest of the world were infected with germs that are artificially preserved only in test-tubes, as if a disease, conquered and wiped out in its place of origin, has escaped from the petri dish and is spreading itself throughout the world. How wonderful it would be if the American city planners were to confront themselves with the questions of responsibility, if they were to at least face up to them, seeing that their European colleagues are too busy living in the media and as a logo. How wonderful it would be if they were to consider that now, more than ever, their influence on the rest of the world could be the determining factor. We know how much architecture and the canons of the Greek city have influenced the Latin world. Athens was well known for "civilizing" the barbarian Romans through its own models of beauty and meaning. Today America and Europe are not in a comparable exalted position to take on the parallel task of influencing the way of life in African, Asian, and Latin

American cities. Still, the influence is there, and it is the influence of the dead ideas of skyscrapers, superblocks, and shopping malls. Even a city such as the new Korean capital Songdo, which sets itself up to be only a hub, is nothing but a string of towers, superhighways and settings for consumerism. Taking all this to be "reality," to be the inevitable reality Rem Koolhaas would have us embrace, gives to the contemporary city a metaphysical dimension that it does not deserve. Therefore, to be "against architecture" nowadays, to deprecate the betrayal of a practice that should be the keystone of a shared, significant built environment is urgent also in America. "Against architecture," because one can no longer put up with the formalism, the tiredness, and the fear that pervade even both architectural studies and productions. This book is an indictment against the laziness of a profession that used to promise a lot and that today is a washout. It's an indictment against those who believe city planners to be the mediators capable of understanding the urgency of a turnaround. This book is the experience of travels made in Italy, France, Portugal, Spain, and Japan, gathered each time with rage, with arguments, but also with the passionate capacity for putting oneself into the midst of the crisis, of responding to the critics with willingness to reform and to reinvent the profession. It is with this spirit that the book comes out in the United States, in the hopes that American architects and city planners, projectors, and designers will know how to go beyond the vague wave of fear that blocks them and keeps them hostage to the brand of the past and that they will throw themselves into inventing a new world of community living, of streets and houses, of cities and landscapes.

CHAPTER 1

Why I Did Not Become an Architect

> Le Corbusier, for example, may design the most health-giving, labour-saving, altogether desirable residences; but he is no more an architect than a planner of up-to-date and equally (from the hens' point of view) desirable hen-houses.
> —Robert Byron, *The Appreciation of Architecture* (1932)

WHY DIDN'T I BECOME AN ARCHITECT?

Really, why, in spite of my interest in cities and the built environment and the way they enfold the generations who occupy them, did I not continue my architectural studies? Actually, I really did become an architect, but then I began to be troubled, I had qualms that prevented my going forward, my being an architect, my doing it as a career. For years I asked myself why on earth this avoidance was such a sure, precise thing, even if I never felt it was something personal. It was not my choice; it was an inevitable choice. So why instead did I become someone who writes, someone who writes about cities, about spaces, about life in those spaces? This year, for the first time, I no longer felt myself alone. In a Paris bookshop I discovered a recent book by Orhan Pamuk, *Other Colours,* and in it I found an essay entitled "Why I Did Not Become an Architect."[1] I hadn't known that Pamuk, a cultivated and disturbing writer from the ephemeral and complex world of Istanbul, who has won the Nobel Prize in Literature, with his temperament suspended between Constantinople and Istanbul, had also started out studying architecture. Then something happened to him. Having to search for a space to rent or buy in the old Galata quarter, he was drawn in, willy-nilly, as he visited dozens of occupied apartments: in big houses, constructed by Armenian, Greek, Jewish, and Genoese merchants and craftsmen, their silent entryways infused with worlds of intimacy, scenes of everyday life. At the top of the double staircases that led up from the lobby, apartments opened up that had been carved out from many little divisions of these mercantile houses, salons of another Istanbul, more cosmopolitan, more tolerant than now. The writer found himself looking into rooms occupied by children stretched out on old divans watching TV, by seniors reading the newspaper in the kitchen, by strapping women with the questioning air of those subjected to an intrusion but at the same time puzzled by the presence of a stranger. The everyday life that consumed and filled these rooms conceived for other stories and other lives, the replenishment of the space in these old mansions with the more modest but insistent and trivial minutiae of today, the customs, the fumes, the sounds of the kitchen, and the odors of washing and ironing. After having traversed so many lives and followed so many corridors and having spied on and been spied on by the occupants of so many rooms, the reasons for architecture began to fade and then disappeared altogether. Had he actually entered the architectural field, he would have designed, projected, planned, but he would never have had anything to do with this kind of reality but rather something faraway, abstract, and quite contrary to the dimension of daily Istanbul life. He would have planned apartment blocks, flats in multistory blocks like those that proliferate in the suburbs of the city, but it would have been impossible for him to have anything to do with real houses. Because houses are the outcome of the confused, fragmentary, rough-and-ready arrangements that constitute living, Pamuk never really puts it like that—"living"—the whole essay says something indecipherable and precise at the same time. What clouds the vision and makes it frustrating, indeed, useless to be an architect, is the way that the reality of occupied spaces, branded and scarred with use, compares with the perception of them. If I have understood correctly, the question is that architecture knows nothing of that precisely narrative essence from which spaces are made. Pamuk became a writer, because that makes more sense; it is more honest in facing the way his city is made up. He wants to bear witness to this city, he wants to be present in it, gathering with a sharp eye and witty shrewdness the past of places, of events, of its stones. Better to write, to narrate, because places don't stand still, they change with the swelter of the lives that leave their imprints there, with the elusive approximation of intrinsicality. Before encountering Pamuk as a soul mate, I had not understood the relationship between not becoming an architect and instead becoming a writer. It seemed to me that the two things were not connected, that writing was an original, archetypical passion that had replaced my attention to the built environment. Instead, during the course of my writing life, space again injected itself forcefully and, along with it, living spaces and spaces designed by architects. I became close again to architects, or rather, to tell the truth, they became close to me, irritated and upset as they were by my criticisms of them. And with some of them, on various, ever more frequent occasions, I started a frank, open discussion, with the proviso that there be a willingness on their part to join in wholeheartedly and not close themselves off behind the security of their profession. But only through Pamuk did I understand how for me, as for him, writing is the most honest way to deal with the city and with space, because writing does not kill magmaticity, nor presume to invent it, nor expect to exhaust it. Writing keeps in step, it cherishes the stones and the people who live with them, it speaks of the process through which the stones and the people mingle with one another. That which elsewhere I have called the "local frame of mind," a personal and collective history where spaces and territories are indistinguishable from the experience one has with them over the course of time. That is, it is something that can be defined only by storytelling.

Writing is very likely writing about this: there is no distinction between descriptions of landscapes, of urban and nonurban geographies, and of real life experiences. The geography of the novel is not a juxtaposition of disciplines but is an indispensable key to understanding the novel *and* the geography. We unravel time in rooms and the rooms help us to recover and rewind the thread of time. It is for this reason, if I have understood Pamuk properly, that one cannot do less than renounce architecture, because architecture has nothing to do with the substance of the true geography of the present. This book, the umpteenth on lived-in and constructed space, wishes only to make one little point. Until such time as the city and the practices put into motion for understanding it and transforming it abandon the burden of the stroke-of-genius reformers of which architecture today seems to be the most fashionable representative; until such time as they take back being first and foremost the narration, the clarification of the profound and dense galaxy, of the existential horizontal and vertical configuration in which cities are made, there will be only useless exercises, caprices of so-called creative types kissed on a sterile backstage by the Fates of fashion.

⟝

Shopping is arguably the last remaining form of public
activity.

—Rem Koolhaas

Strolling around New York, another city of layers like Istanbul, a
city of continuous demolition and contemporary aging, perhaps
older than Istanbul, if age be measured in things consumed by
obsolescence; strolling and looking at the new architecture of
Frank Gehry, Renzo Piano, Koolhaas, SANAA, I read with an
architect friend an article by Nicolai Ouroussoff in the *New
York Times* (December 23, 2007): "Manhattan's Year of Building
Furiously."

> New York's embrace of architecture has a dark side. . . .
> The majority of today's projects serve the interests of a
> small elite. And this trend is not likely to change any time
> soon. The slow death of the urban middle class, the rise
> of architecture as a marketing tool, the overweening influ-
> ence of developers—all have helped to narrow architec-
> ture's social reach just as it begins to recapture the public
> imagination. From this perspective the wave of gorgeous
> new buildings can be read as a mere cultural diversion.
>
> Additionally, New York is about to embark on a hand-
> ful of vast developments that could alter its character
> more than any other projects since the 1960s. Twenty-five
> million square feet of commercial space is planned for
> Midtown [and] Madison Square Garden. . . . An enor-
> mous expansion of the Columbia University campus into
> Harlem has enraged the local residents [who are threat-
> ened with mass expulsion]. And let's not forget Ground
> Zero, a black hole of political posturing, cynical real
> estate deals, and outright stupidity.

Never so much as this year is there such talk of architecture in
New York. Constructions just completed or in the planning
stage are multiplying: Renzo Piano presented the city with the

expansion of the Morgan Library and the skyscraper for the *New York Times*; SANAA have finished their strange minimalist museum in the Bowery, which looks like something out of a Muji shop-window; Frank Gehry has a new building near the meatpacking district, the IAC Headquarters building—without the usual metal swirls, it plays with wrapped glass in two colors (the same idea that characterizes the new prison in San Francisco, a work, however, designed by an obscure architect); Diller Scofidio in the same area are working on a linear park on a disused railway line; Ground Zero is still in the midst of an argument even after the supersimplification of Daniel Libeskind's plan was scotched by the realtors. All this, however, has little to do with the city; it is a window-dressing debate that will result in the transformation of Manhattan into a brand, into a platform star-studded with architectural monuments to consumerism like the entire shopping system to which the city is perilously close to reducing itself.

Because of this, Pamuk returns to mind: beyond the architectural debate, beyond the same awareness of the absolutely antisocial character of this new architecture and of this idea of the city, what has all this to do with the real way in which cities live, with cities as complex and living organisms? Nothing. All this is irrelevant. Certainly, masses of people will be pushed out elsewhere, Manhattan will lose the varied and popular character that it had maintained for decades after the war, and life will spring up somewhere else, where the inhabitants will have more space to experiment and reconstruct themselves. And debating architecture will remain sterile and useless because cities are made from a different mixture. Of course it can be interesting for the fans of the various "archistars," to use the term coined by Gabriella Lo Ricco and Silvia Micheli in their brilliant book, to see who will best represent the transformation of Manhattan into a capital of shopping and brands, with the illusion of a bright and aware postmodernity.[2] Charles Jencks predicts in his latest book, *Critical Modernism*, that a "critical modernism" could move ahead, but the impression is that all this is of interest only for a world of workaholics, a world of collectors.[3] On the other hand—and beyond a certain facile cynicism—is it not really in this sense that one can read Rem Koolhaas's declaration that the only space reserved for the citizenry today, the only way to express democratic participation, is shopping?

> The central question is whether architects who in their
> work try to resist and criticize the norms of the general
> contemporary culture/society, are engaged in a futile and
> self-deluding activity.
>
> —William S. Saunders[4]

One night, sleeping in an old loft on Fifth Street, I was awakened by the noise of the pipes—yelling, screaming pipes. I had no idea what it was, but it seemed as if the entire building itself was complaining in its bones, blaming its rheumatism. Piercing noises of levers, of wrenches banging on lead and tin. They explained to me the next day that it was actually a matter of the old heating pipes that contract, expand, dilate, weaken, and separate into creaking segments. New York is extremely old, as only modernity can be, another theme of which the architects are enamored—Koolhaas scolds his colleagues for not being modern enough, as, for example, the Chinese, who have no scruples about building millions of cubic feet, because modernity is mass, bigness, enormous hugeness, speed. Nevertheless, modernity is finished, and it long ago retired into its old age and departed in its own fashion, and the architects are merely prolonging the agony for their shady professional motives. New York is layered with old stratification, with constant conflict between the wide city sidewalks, three or four yards wide, and that ultimate unsuitability, the skyscraper, completely unsuited for living in, but which nonetheless has to be inhabited. New York is made of other dimensions, those of the Bowery, the Lower East Side, and even the decorous West Side Midtown. A city of nineteenth-century Egyptian, deco, and Liberty styles, with streetlights that nail the evening sky to the sidewalk; with an average height of two stories, the "stoops," the stone steps leading up to the house, built to avoid flooding. This is New York living, in a city surrounded by water. Without the street and its force of attraction toward lower heights, skyscrapers would not exist. It is street life that allows the skyscraper to be what it is. Houses and streets that maintain, even in the presence of the skyscrapers, that vertigo is possible only by returning everything to a horizontal dimension; the daily round of the New Yorker, who never looks up, but feels the exhilaration in gravity. Skyscrapers are a paradox. It's the street life that allows them to set themselves off, a life that now for the first time is really destined to disappear in order to give place to an external image, brand named, for the tourists. Tourists come to New York so they can feel modern, to buy into the illusion of modernity, that delirium extolled by Koolhaas that has been over for quite some time.

New York says what the architects don't want to hear, and that is that their work is practically useless—as far as making a city goes—that what they do is sell a two-dimensional monumentality or, in the best of cases, wrench from their clients a stamped consent for limited containers of public space. To be sure, it is not an easy game. I talk with Kenneth Frampton who sings me the praises of the new extension to the Morgan Library by Renzo Piano. Out of the blue, a very private institution allows an architect the liberty of opening up a covered corridor inside a city block. Here one feels as if in a greenhouse between the houses, a little peephole on the backyards. Sitting in the sterile café that they have installed in it, one might suspect that maybe all of Manhattan could be like this, that it would be possible to make hundreds of spaces like this. But one also has the impression that the game is rapidly being sucked into the new mentality of control that nowadays dominates the city. These are spaces to be enjoyed under the watchful eyes of a whole team of vigilantes. Forget freedom of movement in the area! Raise your eyes to the heights that Piano has created, to the huge jutting terrace suspended over the elevator and your heads, and you will quickly spot a guard who is watching to make sure you don't do something untoward.

It is a sign of life, a sign of community, in part, to justify in a politically correct manner the public function of a gigantic private collection. In reality, it would be beautiful if from here one could leave on another more ambitious journey; if the architects had wanted to be a class of enthusiasts for the beauty of the city and for living there; if they were intellectuals who despised the mediocrity, the showcasing, the plasticification of everyday life. They would perhaps have more influence like that, as groups of lovers of urban beauty, rather than as designers of monumental objects or of porcelain for collectors. Right now, however, we are at the opposite end. Far from representing the troubled conscience of neocapitalist real estate, architects today are, generally speaking, adolescent hobbyists who are selling themselves as public artists.

> The publicized architect, the "archistar" springs from the entwining of the processes embedded in the traditional critical texts which have never been rescinded. Therefore the fundamental elements which are the basis of the burgeoning fame of architects have been looked into and characterized; a compendium of data and hidden facts, which come to light between the lines of the biographies, in the interstices of the writings of the same authors, in the recurring motives that repeat from one phenomenon to another, through the connections which bring to life the so-called dynamics.
>
> —Gabriella Lo Ricco, Silvia Micheli, *Lo spettacolo dell'architettura, profilo dell'archistar*

With Emiliano Armani, who, unlike me, decided to become an architect, I embarked on a journey to the Bronx. I wanted to convince him that, contrary to current thinking, the Bronx is a world of vital worlds, a quarter where the declining Manhattan life was now moving. Loretta D'Orsogna, an Italian researcher who was born and grew up in the Bronx, has described in a singular guide to the Bronx all the things that one can seek and find there: the Zoo, pristine nature, magnificent art deco architecture, boulevards, plus an attachment to the place.[5] A significant reorganization of the community had taken place there and was continuing to take place. The day was freezing and an icy wind swept through the streets. We took refuge in a Neapolitan-Mexican pizzeria where we slurped down some hot soup. With our courage refortified, we found ourselves at one of the fundamental crossroads of the Bronx, Fordham Road and Grand Concourse. Shops full of gaudy clothes, which only the Latinas, balancing on their giddily high heels, could get away with, taquerias, stores with Latin rhythm, shops with crocodile shoes produced in Italy for the public here. Yes, and in all of it there was joy, confusion, rhythm, and present-day architecture, made by people, local people—and lots of action on the sidewalk. Nothing special, but here was public space that no trumped-up place in Manhattan could ever compete with. It came to mind that where there is life there is luckily forgetfulness on the part of the shotgun administrators like Giuliani, like the mayor of New York, Bloomberg, about planning all mixed in with real estate profits and architectural superstars.[6] In the Bronx one can still savor that mosaic of which once upon a time Manhattan was the world symbol, a city of Babel, a feverish daily confusion. Today one could almost believe Marc Augé: Manhattan produces places without place, boxes of glass and tin whose intentionality can give nothing to the passers-by and the inhabitants, obeying to the end the technique of Giuliani, the ex-mayor who decided that in order to clean up the boroughs it was necessary to punish all the small-time crooks, which resulted in cleaned-up squares devoid of any of the informal activities that coexisted as part of its fabric. Today even the street-people have to beg pardon, or find a disguise so as not to disturb the general décor.

> We are now at the beginning of an era whose construc-
> tions are far scarier than ruins. In the time of which I
> write, the new silicon-based life forms were sneaking
> into every interstice without setting off alarms that all
> would be utterly changed in a way far more insidious
> than nuclear war, that they would bring a new wealth that

would erase the ruins. In the 1980s we imagined apoca-
lypse because it was easier than the strange complicated
futures that money, power, and technology would impose,
intricate futures hard to exit.[7]

Another hot soup, this time in a taqueria in the Bronx. As soon as
we begin to speak Spanish to the girl behind the counter everything changes, the neighborhood offers us its services: do we
want a car to drive around in? A Cuban friend to explain to us
where to find the best mole poblano? We warm ourselves at the
juke-box with "cantares durangueños y rancheros." Emiliano
has brought along *A Field Guide to Getting Lost,* the recent book
by Rebecca Solnit, whose cult book *Wanderlust,* (translated
into Italian as *Storia del Camminare*) we both admire.[8] I asked
Kenneth Frampton if he knew her; I consider her one of the
sharpest minds with regard to the city, the environment, history.
No, but it's par for the course that he doesn't know of her: architecture, even among its most cultured personalities, is a world
that reads only what is strictly defined by the discipline of architecture, rather like art critics. We discover the pages in which
Rebecca Solnit talks about ruin. She describes her punk adoles-
cence in San Francisco, and how for her and her contemporaries the city was full of forgotten spaces, of abandoned industrial
architecture.

Coming of age in the heyday of punk, it was clear we were
living at the end of something—of modernism, of the
American Dream, of the industrial economy, of a certain
kind of urbanism. The evidence was all around us in the
ruins of the cities. The Bronx was block after block, mile
after mile of ruin, as were even some Manhattan neighborhoods, housing projects across the country were in a
state of collapse, many of the shipping piers which had
been key to San Francisco's and New York's economies
were abandoned, as was San Francisco's big Southern

Pacific rail yard and its two most visible breweries. Vacant lots like missing teeth gave a tough grin to the streets we haunted. Ruin was everywhere, for cities had been abandoned by the rich, by politics, by a vision of the future. Urban ruins were the emblematical places for this era, the places that gave punk part of its aesthetic, and like most aesthetics, this one contained an ethic, a worldview with a mandate on how to act, how to live.

What is a ruin, after all? A human construction abandoned to nature, and one of the allures of ruins in the city is that of wilderness: a place full of the promise of the unknown with all its epiphanies and dangers. Cities are built by men (and to a lesser extent, women), but they decay by nature, from earthquakes and hurricanes to the incremental processes of rot, erosion, rust, the microbial breakdown of concrete, stone, wood, and brick.

For Rebecca Solnit, the poetical punk, it was the idea that only the abandoned city, the forgotten city, could acquire oblivion, descend into unconsciousness. The ruins are what remains of the city, left over, neglected, set aside when the intentions of the planners, the administrators and the architects cease to exist. (On the other hand, once the project is completed they, the latter especially, totally abandon the construction to its fate.) They are the ones convinced of being the conscious part of the city and of returning it to a state of awakening and light. But cities are above all insensate; they "fall" into unconsciousness rather quickly, whether one wants them to or not, and it is in this state that they come to be lived in. Rebecca continues:

> A city is built to resemble a conscious mind, a network that can calculate, administrate, manufacture. Ruins become the unconscious of a city, its memory, unknown, darkness, lost lands, and in this truly bring it to life. With ruins a city springs free of its plans into something as

intricate as life, something that can be explored, but perhaps not mapped. This is the same transmutation spoken of in fairy tales when statues and toys and animals become human, though they come to life and with ruin a city comes to death, but a generative death like the corpse that feeds flowers. An urban ruin is a place that has fallen outside the economic life of the city, and it is in some way an ideal home for the art that also falls outside the ordinary production and consumption of the city.[9]

Living is the direct communication between the subconscious of the city and the subconscious of the inhabitants. This brings us again to "local frame of mind." But because "local frame of mind" is an expression that still implies a certain state of consciousness, whereas what is working here is not a thought but, as Richard Sennett would say, "flesh and stone." The dream flesh of which we are made is the same dream stone into which the cities will sooner or later crumble.

Architects have no idea of all this, they are convinced that they are putting their hands on the city, but their works are swallowed up by the indifference of shopping and the magnificent voraciousness of the collective unconscious (which rarely comes in the form that the architects imagine, inexpert as they are in the complexity of the symbolic system that unites city and inhabitants). Emiliano and I therefore finished by telling ourselves that the questions in which the architects are embroiled are for the most part irrelevant or badly posited. If Koolhaas wants to work himself up to demonstrate the need for still being modern "without making too many problems for oneself," he needs to ask himself why being modern is such an objective. Cities have never been modern, one could say, paraphrasing Bruno Latour. There is however another element in the words of Rebecca Solnit that is apropos for us. Because she also talks about art, and of the context of art, and of the conditions thanks to which art can find a place.

> Architecture is the most universal of the arts. It enshrines
> the past in a form more extensive, more varied, and more
> easily apprehensible that any other form of culture. It
> exhibits the taste and aspirations of the present to all who
> traverse the streets of a city and raise their eyes as they go.
> Paintings are in galleries; literature in books. The galler-
> ies must be visited, the books opened. But buildings are
> always with us. Democracy is an urban thing, and archi-
> tecture is its art.
>
> —Robert Byron, *The Appreciation of Architecture* (1932)

And if the architects were nothing but artists? Why impute
to them a responsibility they don't have? At the end of the
day, as Massimiliano Fuksas maintained in an interview in *La
Repubblica* (January 22, 2008), the problem is political: the politicians have to combat the inequality of distribution that afflicts
the cities, it's up to the politicians to confront the general emergency in which we live. Architects busy themselves with other
things, formal beauty, décor, in short, precious things. In one way
or another, this is the constant alibi of the past twenty years. The
architects produce the "icing on the cake," even if more and more
their work is a requisite for the marketing of products, of brand
names, of fashion houses or of tourism or the showbiz agencies
for whom they are working. In short, the archistars are nothing more than the service artists of today's powers, useful for
establishing "trends," to amaze and draw the public's attention
with "gimmicks" that are not even buildings but stage sets, like
enormous billboards crumpled up to form museums, branches
of communications agencies, and some spectacular Disney-fied
quarters. Why get mixed up with them? In effect they are doing
the work of a humble modern artist, playing with forms and
formations in the space allotted to them, nothing more than a
formal exercise, a gymnastic maintenance of good taste. Why get
mixed up with Frank Gehry, who released statements in favor
of his best client, the multimillionaire Paul Allen of Microsoft,

who played a major role in the Enron scandal, and for whom he had designed the Experience Music Project of Seattle? What interests us more here, however, is the new type of artist who is born of personalities like Gehry. To quote the bible of corporate creativity, *New Ideas about New Ideas* by Shira White and G. Patton Wright:

> In this new age . . . innovation can only come from people and organizations that are "hot, hip, and happening." Since nowadays "the artist is more valued than the manager," business leaders must become more like artists, must look to artists as models in both their personal and professional lives. Naturally Frank Gehry is the artist who stands above all others in such a hierarchy, thanks especially to his work for the art-appreciating insurance magnate Peter Lewis and for the brand-building Guggenheim chain of museums.[10]

And the book goes on until the Enron case: a corporation cited as one that best assimilated this lesson.

In short, the architect is an artist, but in a renewed sense he is more than anything a "trend-setter," someone like Koolhaas, who opened new marketing directions for Prada, furnishing not only the surroundings, but also a completely new spirit in the company. In a show-business economy the artist becomes the key element, capable of producing the setting that the show needs to move forward. If it is true, as David Harvey says, that capitalism has been saved by the real estate business, it is also true that we find ourselves at present in a more advanced stage: today we are being redeemed by the application of the creative arts to the production of trends, styles, surfaces, ceremonial images. The archistar does not work for fashion; he has become fashion, with the brand, the logo, a warranty of power to sign a part of the city, a museum, a shop, an island in Dubai, as if it were a t-shirt. In a post-Debordian perspective: not only has art become pure spectacle but it is even more dematerialized by becoming the illusion of the creative spark, with the possibility of acquiring its atmosphere, its allure.

The architect drops his mantle over the city to make sure that it is "his way," truly contemporary, truly fixed in the trends that form the "happening," the frame of the event. Except then he shuts himself off, as Fuksas does, in the alibi of not having any responsibility, of being only a humble artist[11], an artisan who at the most could say, "Let's leave the problems to those who have to take care of them." On the other hand, wasn't that the answer that Mies van der Rohe gave, well into Nazism, when he was accused of being a collaborator? "Artists have always worked for those in power, why are you surprised?" Few remember that Mies promised Nazism to present them with a new Bauhaus, cleansed of its Jewish infestations, and that when he made up his mind to leave Germany for the United States, he did it because he had lost the competition for the reconstruction of Berlin, which the Führer had decided to assign to his little pal Albert Speer.[12] In a word, the plot of the old movie *Mephisto*.

> [On the one hand,] there has never been a more propitious moment than now to revisit the question of architecture's social responsibilities, [but on the other hand,] the gap that exists between the specialized discourses of planning, architecture, political process, and the public has never been so great.
>
> —Anthony Vidler[13]

> There are sort of rules about architectural expression which have to fit into a certain channel. Screw that! It doesn't mean anything. I am going to do what I do the best and if it's no good the marketplace will deny it.
>
> —Frank Gehry[14]

A lecture given by Joseph Rykwert at the Alvar Aalto Foundation in Helsinki in 2001 was entitled "Is Architecture Still Good for the City?" Rykwert maintained that even the masters of the Modern

Movement such as Walter Gropius dreamed of a transformation of the profession into a managerial form capable of managing property deals: the architect as the coordinator of the world of real estate. Rykwert quoted current figures from Transparency International, a nongovernmental agency concerned with world corruption. According to this agency, the construction business is responsible for 78 percent of corruption in the world (on the other hand, one should read Robert Saviano's *Gomorra* to learn more about the preeminence of the Camorra in trafficking in the building trade, and it was not by chance that the Gambino family was involved with the "Ground Zero Affair"). According to Rykwert, notwithstanding these facts, the architect can and could still have an extraordinary democratic function and could be the point of contact for those who are attempting to construct the ideal city. He could be, simply because his profession is centered on thinking of the city, of having knowledge of an intimate connection with the richness of its history, an intellectual milieu particularly sensitive to the degeneration of both the built and the natural environment. Elsewhere Rykwert singles out the dearth in contemporary architecture of the capacity to produce shared symbols, and for having reduced the symbolic system of the constructed world to an elementary level. And he refers to the example of the competition for Ground Zero, to the paucity of ideas offered, even by Libeskind's plan. It's hard to believe that the only method of putting together a wounded city lies in such a banal conception of reconstruction as "let's build it like it was before, but even higher," as if the skyscraper could explain through its own erection the aspiration of millions of people towards a serene and peaceful life.

~✤

This city, loved since childhood,
in its December peace seems to me today
to be a squandered inheritance.

—Anna Akhmatova

Cities dream of other cities. This evidence assailed me in St. Petersburg last summer. A surprise to discover that Venice dreamed of a place other than itself, a city similar in its modernity, its canals, its lagoon, its bridges, and its neighborhoods. Of course, there was Peter the Great, of course there was the state of magniloquence of the monarchy in the century when it could still be believed in. That the red porphyry city cost thousands of victims, the forced labor of hundreds of thousands of hands, a massacre of underlings, all this I know. But the power of Peter was a dream that he transformed into a nightmare. It took a hundred years to cleanse the city from the great poets and writers who decried its underlying malign aspect, and then it took the terrible siege by the Nazis, and then it took the famine. Still, the Petersburg redeemed and stealthily praised by Akhmatova, is already a clean dream, the dream of a city whose beauty is its soul, its stones become the echoes of intentions, waves of intelligence. A city where one wants to say: well, I would like to live here, because here in this place there is something stronger than its individual buildings and its monuments. No, this city wasn't born only through the planning of the tsarist Empire. No, there was a dream of a city that was created in Europe from Venice onwards, a city in which it would be worthwhile to live; places of porticos and bridges, of streets and alleyways, a complex of windows, a stratagem of ways. The stones allude to other stones. Often this happens to cities, to feel themselves only the shadow of other places, or to cast their shadow on still other places.

What is it about St. Petersburg? Its urbanity, an inkling of the crowd and the individual, it has classic stone, a colonnade, a dimension. This summer I reread Rykwert's *The Dancing Column*,[15] and I don't know if I have understood it, but Petersburg is still a city that nurtures itself on the human dimension of the column, on the classical discourse of its orders, orders that "incite" the city, that make it arise from a simple assemblage of trabeations and columns, architraves and doorways. Perhaps it is the last classical city, and it is a classical city pushed into modernity. Perhaps the only cities in which one could dream of living are those that seize the column as its form of human prototype. So I think of classical New York, a late romantic city of little old ladies and detectives, of fogs and wind, of darkness and cones of light reflected from street-lights. Why was humankind able to create cities for centuries, knowing what to do, putting together a simple work of assembling the elements? Perhaps because these elements had a unifying force that went beyond the single architectonic genius or the single-minded arrogance of power. The imperial cities were cities with an order that certainly was submissive to the Emperor but that in some manner preexisted him.

For Petersburg the situation is paradoxical. In the early years of the twentieth century the tsar is still closed inside his rooms of cupids and arcadia. For the powerful this was the classic trap, a mythology secure for centuries, a laic-pagan mythology as a counterpoint to clerical ideology and the spasms of the revolutionaries of the millenarian sects. When everything collapses with the fall of the classical gods, the city does not collapse. It resists by its urbanity, holds on to a style, a "way of life," really in a Wittgenstein sense, something that predates all intentions, a practice made up of the inveterate stubbornness of curves and straight lines, of levels that overlook one another, the glimpses of gardens, and the onion-shaped trees. How do we account for this grand history of dreams, of Venice, which is dreaming of Istanbul, which is dreaming of Moscow? Today when we talk of Empire, of Global Power, nothing could be further from the sensation that this global Empire knew how to take on a "way of life" capable of creating a city. In Moscow I found an incredible issue of a contemporary Russian review of architecture. It was a monographic issue, dedicated to "Capitalist

Realism," a style the editors identified with huge new residential projects: I had seen them, immense blocks of flats making a wall towards the Gulf of Finland, in a colored "Chippendale" style, so many gigantic beehives sweetened with a neoplastic façade as if Philip Johnson or Robert Venturi had left some little sketches lying around without saying how much they were to be enlarged.

This capitalist realism is flooding all of Russia, and taking over the features of entire quarters in the new central Asiatic capitals. It is a residential monumentality that recalls that of Stalin, with moreover a note of cynicism, of cynical irony. It is the style of many of the new buildings in Dubai, as well as the general style of many Chinese buildings; a massive style filtered through the awareness of design, scrollwork on the fashionable apartment building: a kind of immense victorious Bofill. I don't know if all that constitutes a city. I don't think so. I see the dreams, but they are dreams from realism to realism, dreams of a power that has lost structure and substituted itself for it. It's as if politics—state and planning politics, the politics of Bulgakov's *Heart of a Dog*, which supposedly should produce the new man by wrenching him out of humanity—were to believe that the structure of a city could correspond to the structure of power. But it's not like that, I know it's not like that.

> The retina is the point of sale: to see is to buy. In contem-
> porary "casino capitalism," citizenship is a credit line,
> democracy a crapshoot.
>
> —Michael Sorkin

I'm fed up with this Manhattan, where the only movement seems to be that of Italian ants scurrying to Victoria's Secret to buy lingerie for their wives, yokels who are convinced that *Sex and the City* is a sexual revolution. I'm sick of window-shopping that is unconvincing, sick of a grandeur that reflects the idea that Europeans have of "Bigness." Ah, Bigness, what a magnificent new slogan, dear Rem Koolhaas; as if it is sufficient to turn every-thing into a logo so that it suddenly becomes real. Who knows whether in Dutch "actueel" has the same meaning as "actual" has in English. It would be interesting if behind realism there was something real, "the real thing," the proper thing, the thing that is wanted. Not perhaps the perfect thing, but the thing that is wanted, it would be interesting if it were part of your constel-lation. But no, the actuality of Bigness is in the same category as the logos, to which it feels good to say YE$, thinking of Yen, Euro, Dollar, just as it also came into your mind to change the flag of the European Union into a barcode. But the realism of which you are the happy discoverer is not what is wanted, but what it is. In short, I know that all that is real is rational and you are the master of reminding your colleagues and the culture that everything has a healthy realism: and that realism is corpora-tions, branding, shopping, real estate. (If one didn't know that "realty" and "reality" have two different origins it would make me very happy if you were to write them on a placard—that I know REAL(I)TY, or better, R.E.A.L.(I).T.Y.)

One of your faithful disciples defines your work like this:

> His investigative attitude—toward New York in the 1920s
> and 1930s, toward Atlanta and Singapore in the 1980s,
> toward Lagos, China, and shopping in the 1990s, and

> toward historic preservation in the 2000s—has spread
> widely among young architectural thinkers, as well it
> should have. . . . [In] the mid-1990s many highly intel-
> ligent architects and architectural intellectuals were
> getting fed up with this detachment, theoretical abstrac-
> tion, and helplessness. They wanted to (and could, with
> an improved economy) get to work on real projects, real
> conditions, real places; they wanted to be ambitious with-
> out being dreamy, to improve bits of the world without
> self-aggrandizing delusions.[16]

At this point the profession had already changed enormously.
The market required another type of figure, such as Frank Gehry
had started to put forward in his works. Kevin Ervin Kelley, a
marketing and creativity expert, considering his works, defined
the new professional figure in an article entitled *Architecture for
Sale(s)*, harking back to Cole Porter's song "Love for Sale." Just
avoid a little ambiguity, and everything becomes very clear:

> Calling what our firm does "architecture" was quite
> confusing for all involved, so we redesigned our service as
> "Perception Design,"—we help prompt consumers to buy
> through environmental "signaling" that influences their
> perceptions. In a sense, we are designing the consum-
> ers themselves. Brand cueing takes place in the built
> elements, but also the menu, uniforms, logo, aromas, and
> music, plus sensations, and, most important, emotions.
> Most architects are surprised that our firm generally
> won't take on a project unless we are involved in evaluat-
> ing all the elements of the brand.[17]

When I ran into Koolhaas in Bordeaux, at the *Mutations* Expo,
which under the auspices of Stefano Boeri and Hans Ulrich
Obrist, was a fair that welcomed contributions from groups dedicated to the "resistance" of globalization and of "public architecture" but which devolved immediately to sustaining the esthetic

of the new archistars, one of the things that amazed me about
him was the use he made of the misery of the world. There was
a video in which an architect, I believe it was actually he, was
commenting on the demolition of a slum. Tractors and bull-
dozers were sweeping away the miserable hovels with people
in front of them, people who had scarcely had time to get out. I
believe that I decided then and there that there was something
rotten about all this. How was it possible that Koolhaas's intelligent realism could lead to this? Was it not terrifying to use
the misery of the world just to demonstrate how up-to-date he
was, how really ahead of everyone? And then was it certain that
Koolhaas and the curators of the exhibition really understood
anything about the misery of the world? Wasn't their prettifying of the catastrophe at the end of the day a prettifying of cynicism? Everything that was on display in that exhibition—I had
brought a video shot with Stefano Savona on Tunisian immigrants in Sicily, of Stalker's own experience with streetwalk-
ers in the suburbs—everything was ground up in the cauldron,
a patched-together esthetic, superficial, magazine-like, based
on "hip" operations. A friend, Laura Ruggieri, who lives and
teaches in Hong Kong, and who continues to speak out about
the California-zation of the Pearl River, has talked with me at
length about these things. She is a militant who fights against
evictions, the destruction of the popular fabric, what's left of it,
of Hong Kong. She has rented a shop-front, saved from the over-
zealous clean sweep, and installed herself there to communicate
with the people, to communicate that in some fashion one can
resist this overzealousness. But she has never turned this into
an artistic happening. She told me: "No, the idea that one could
make an esthetic out of resistance, out of political action, out of
being against the horrors of real estate, is a Nazi idea. Nazism is
the transformation of politics into an esthetic, and I as an artist
refuse to use the misery of the world as a means to my ends."
Sorry Rem, I know that you are slippery on this point of view.
It's not that you uphold the things you uphold. Your thinking

is elusive, pragmatic, realistic, up-to-date, but forgive me if I permit myself to say that *Mutations* made me a little nauseous. And then obviously I was fascinated by your attention to Dubai in *Al Manakh*: what genius, to have grasped that that is where they are making the world, there where there is the most totally inequitable distribution of means. And there within the framework of the most brutal ideology of imitating the West, with skyscrapers but without democracy, one could erect futuristic villages, millions of tons of cement for new Malibus on the Red Sea, the true dream of "Casino Capitalism," fascinated by the capacity you have for studying Casino Capitalism, of being more realistic than Casino Capitalism itself.

What was it that really made me feel bad about *Mutations*, if not its application of the principles of advertising? To cite a pamphlet quoted by Thomas Frank, "Advertising is a means of contributing meaning and values that are necessary and useful to people in structuring their lives, their casual relationships, and their rituals."[18]

Mutations furnished the advertising viewpoint, in the wake of *S, M, L, XL* and *Shopping*, meanings bestowed from the latest disaster of the world, esthetic and glamorous books through which we interpret injustices and misery. In short, the world as problem had the right to enter into upper-class drawing rooms and insiders' studios. A professional class known for being as resistant to reading as it is prone to riffling through magazines has finally found its intellectual guru, who tells the world its tragedies in a bright glossy guise: between a chamber pot of design and a minimalist Japanese museum, scenes of slums, degraded suburbs, all with a few captions, in order to give the effect "we're showing you through a window what the world is like." In short, the style of *Domus* rendered to perfection under the management of Boeri, Obrist, and Koolhaas.

The doubt that arises now, now that Koolhaas has entered the lists and become the designer, the city planner, and is no longer the guru of hypermodern realism, is that for him the purpose of all this effort is nothing other than the transformation of himself into a brand. It's not that it's not worth the trouble, but it all says more about how today any intellectual work in the ambit of architecture is an ideological construction of self-advertisement: from the superscale of the maestro raking in commissions in Shanghai, to the subordinate disciple that after much intellectual endeavor awards himself the skyscraper to be built in Milan at Isola. And Koolhaas has said all that clearly:

> Basically I think the discussion about what brands are is held on an incredibly primitive level. Particularly the American perception of what brand is, namely something that is reduced to its essence and can never be changed. I think that is a very limited form of branding. What we have been trying to do with Prada, for instance, is instead of trying to reduce it to its essence, we try to stretch it so that more becomes possible rather than less. And that's exactly the same idea that we are trying to introduce for Europe [with the project for the new logo for the EU]. It extends the repertoire of possibilities instead of shrinking it.[19]

Kenneth Frampton has even suggested that the very essence of Koolhaas's work is implicitly contained in his love for logos:

> This is the implicit corporate brand whereby, copying the acronymic formulation of SOM [Skidmore, Owings & Merrill, one of the first architectural firms to be turned into a corporation and to have enthusiastically espoused the Bloomberg logic of real estate], architectural offices assert their corporate status by adopting logolike initials such as KPF, HOK, NBBJ, and even OMA, with which Koolhaas has promoted his own international operation. In this subliminal sleight of hand, the delirious neo-avant-garde enlarges its scope through assuming the aura of corporate power. (Frampton, *Commodification and Spectacle*, xiv)

And Sorkin is even harsher:

> Just as Koolhaas promotes his own brand with a bliz-
> zard of statistics, photos of the "real" world, and a weary
> sense of globalism's inescapable surfeit and waste as
> the only legitimate field of architectural action the
> New Urbanists—with their megalomaniac formulas of
> uniformity—create their slightly "different" Vegas [and
> Disneylands] of "traditional" architecture based on its
> association with the imagined reality of bygone happi-
> nesses. Their tunes may differ [from those of Koolhaas],
> but both are lyricists for the ideological master narrative
> that validates and celebrates the imperial machine.

Said in less malicious words, Koolhaas, an intelligent and prudent man, albeit an ambitious planner, uses the old defense "we are realists" to confirm the status quo. In short, he washes his hands of it all in the most elegant manner. Maintaining that when all is said and done reality is the destiny of reality, he fixes it in a setting that makes any kind of procedure opportune for him, because it is empty of responsibility, and goes all out on the surface of a decadent esthetic, like smoke from the opium den: in short, what can one do, seeing that the world is the way it is? At least allow me to describe it and maybe if I get out of taking part in the construction of the devastation, it is the only thing to be done. His good luck is that, being an intelligent man, every now and then he can snag himself a high-class project, like the new Seattle Library, even while embroiled in a misadventure like EuraLille. However that may be, we know that what he says has little importance—it is merely advertising, and does not impute any responsibility for what he does.

In the end I have to say: Why is he allowed to put his hands on something as serious as the city, seeing that he demonstrates more and more a knowledge garnered from airports and the jet-set? In short, what does he know about all these cities and what does he know about the people who live in them and give meaning to their own space? Koolhaas has never really lived, for example, the daily life of the Chinese; rather his litany of judgments, hung out to the public with sly and allusive accents in *Junkspace*, is in fact made up only of airport opinions and jet-set gossip, of snobbism about those who don't live in the cities he is talking about, who look at them as if they were a shopping cart full of products. But we know that for archistars cities are only a product. Koolhaas shows a bird's eye view of Lagos in his eloquent video: he sees things in an esthetic dimension, while the daily life history of the metropolis, the adventures of Fela Kuti and his resistance clan, the adventures of survival in spite of everything, escapes him. Between his reading of the city and that offered to us by a writer like Suketu Mehta in his book about Mumbai, *Maximum City,* there is the difference between the man who thinks that Sharm el-Sheikh is Egypt and the man who researches in the books of Nagib Mahfus. But everyone knows architects don't read, they riffle.

At the end of the day at least Koolhaas is amusing, at least he avoids the sniveling of Fuksas and doesn't maintain like Gregotti and Purini that they had pledged to the left when they designed the Zen district in Palermo. At least one can't accuse him of hypocrisy, or postworkman ideologism, etc.

Let's leave the absolution to Sorkin:

> If there's a politics to architects like Gehry and Koolhaas hawking their brands, it doesn't devolve on any arcane issues of representation, or even, exactly, on the degree of complicity with the corporate powers for whom they provide jestering and high-cultural legitimization. Nor would it be right to call them union busters for making a living from a kind of client from whom architects have always made a living. Nor, for that matter, is Rem wrong to recognize—in the manner of Hardt and Negri—that under the regime of the empire of global capital, there is no outside, that there is no approach to the system save from within.

But where *Empire* proposes a politics of resistance, Rem is simply acquiescent, as if nothing were at stake. The advocacy of branding is a sell-out in architecture, reducing its meanings to mere advertising, a fine obliviousness to the larger social implications of architectural practice. No amount of bilious insistence that brand is simply the equivalent of culture and its style of inventing identity can obliterate the transformation. But why rebrand the idea of identity in the first place? Why replace the psychical, cultural, and physical constructs compounded in "identity:" with the language of commercial speech? To control it, of course. Branding is just another excuse for power's concentration at the top. The pathetic spectacle of Rem consulting with a number of "leading European intellectuals" to formulate a strategy for the EU flag is precisely as authoritative as the nine out of ten doctors who recommend Preparation H.[20]

The graver journals retain art critics, musical critics, and literary critics, who make it their business to mould public opinion and to create a demand for good painting, good music, and good literature. Architectural critics, on the other hand, scarcely exist. It is "our architectural correspondent" who catalogues the new developments; and since "our architectural correspondent" is in nine cases out of ten himself an architect, he is forbidden by professional etiquette from any real criticism of his fellow architects' designs.

—Robert Byron, *The Appreciation of Architecture* (1932)

Is it by chance that the only decent book about the archistars, and indeed the word itself, comes from two scholarly Italians? Probably not. The system of Italian fashion has certainly given wings to the brandification of the profession. Architects have understood that the only way to escape anonymity and unfair competitions is to take advantage of the pervasive power of fashion and at the same time its characteristic of constant understatement: how can one ask fashion to be ethical, to feel itself responsible to society? Gabriella Lo Rocco and Silvia Micheli have explained clearly how the launching of not only Gehry and Koolhaas, but also Jean Nouvel, Calatrava, and Fuksas really functioned. Without Prada and Armani none of this would have happened. It is the brand names of fashion that have transformed architecture into fashion, in the most profound meaning of the word, not just for clothes, but for trends, for scenarios and for milieus. Architects have carved out from the system of fashion what artists discovered in the system of galleries, curators, and the art market. For artists, however, it's been essential to become famous in life, above all to create first the personality, then the work, even creating themselves as works. For architects this job has been done without the effort of showcasing. They have taken the place of the signature polo shirt, they have become that polo shirt and that pair of underpants.

This has influenced in no small way how architecture is executed. It's not by chance that we are in a whirlwind of constructions: from Renzo Piano's skyscraper for the *New York Times* to SANAA's museum in the Bowery, to the wrapped-grill Armani building in Tokyo by Fuksas, the "signature knitwear theme" predominates, with a "Portofino" or "Riviera" effect, forcing architecture to become an illustration for "Rakam" or "Mani di fata" knitting magazines.

Architecture becomes a fabric, loosely woven; it loses its volumetric density, it becomes rarified. Jean Nouvel promises lightweight dimensions, large, barely perceptible windows, as much as to say that architecture is two-dimensional, that you have to enter it like the pages of a glossy magazine. Frank Gehry goes into his studio, screws a sheet of paper into a ball and says to his faithful CAD implementers: I want that. Thus is architecture vaporized, rendered evanescent, suggesting that the packaging is more important than the product. Only Calatrava shows some muscle and is actually perfect for automobile commercials.

This evolution of style is the ultimate consequence of the triumph of magazines. Architecture is for riffling through: one should buy the large Phaidon Atlas and display it open in the house, it's very chic, even among the uninitiated. No need to be frightened if the construction doesn't correspond to the space, that the live enjoyment of it is a disappointment, not to mention the disappointment of the consumers. With the devastating concurrence of Chirac, Nouvel transformed two extremely important anthropological museums into glassy jewel boxes, flattening two centuries of anthropology into a long distance sales catalog of "major art." His Quai Branly is the triumph of shopping over the history of civilization, the transmogrification of the worldview into Hermès, or Boulevard des Italiens. How strange that architects don't take into consideration how much they are losing, that the price being paid for the showcase is the end of space and of maneuvering spaces.

I have the impression that what gives me so much trouble in this climate is the same thing on which Kenneth Frampton, Charles Jencks, and Joseph Rykwert all agree in the end: that all this has very little to do with the questions in play, with the real "global issues"—with the serious business of the unlivability of the city, of the depletion of resources, of the overheating of the planet. Architects are completely taken in by their own alibi, and while the ship sinks, they who once had the competency of carpenters are nowadays occupying themselves with paper-hanging: the ship is going down, but the important thing is to seize the last hand in the Casino Capitalism Party Room.

We are also dealing with arrogance here. No one has it in for Gehry like the president emeritus of Boston University, John Silber, who as a competent layman, but also as a client, has written an important book entitled *Architecture of the Absurd: How "Genius" Disfigured a Practical Art.*[21] This book lists all the blunders, all the most monumental errors of the great architects: of Josep Lluis Sert, for example, who worked a lot for Boston University. Sert ignored the environmental conditions, the materials appropriate for the climate and the light of Boston, obsessively following, like a good Catalonian, his own "Mediterranean" dream, forcing the unfortunate users of his works to have to bring about many exacting modifications to them in an attempt to render them less inadequate to real life on a northern campus. But the last straw was Frank Gehry, who in his last work for MIT laboratories, the Stata Center, the heart of their scientific research, completely ignoring the directions of the researchers, boxed them into his onion-inspired dreams and common spaces, of merry curved blackboards, of transparent walls, whereas experiments and research, laboratories and procedures of trial and error require a certain privacy, the ability to close oneself behind a door, the possibility of multiple parallel studies. Certainly Gehry is much resented there, and his genius not at all appreciated. But Silber records another disaster, that for the seat of USIS, of the Center for American culture in Paris, where the costs of the project reached such exorbitant proportions that the client was forced to close the place down almost as soon as it was finished.

All in all, the balance is rather sad: we're watching the fireworks of the geniuses of architecture, but where are those who should normally be taking care of the city's public good, of buildings as "public architecture"?

> By thrusting forward and pushing upward, at whatever
> cost of blasting through, New York has come to be what
> it is. Overwhelming, amazing, exciting, violently alive—a
> wilderness of stupendous experiment."
> —H.I. Brock, *New York Times*, November 3, 1935

Still in New York. Rem Koolhaas's mistake is to have believed that New York really was the capital of modernity; instead it is the fulcrum of classicism, the last attempt of classicism to assimilate its own paradoxes. In the 1920s and 1930s New York was no more modern than Moscow or St. Petersburg in its attempt to broaden the unconscious response to the emerging paroxysm of speed. One could say that all three cities have tried, but at a certain point speed has accelerated and left the cities behind. Life is no longer very much interested in the intoxication of speed. Now speed reminds the subconscious only of danger, fire, earthquake, the violence of the automobile, the dizziness of destruction and of self-destruction. New York today is frightening, and it is not the fear engendered by September 11, but the fear of all this scrap iron, this system of pipes, this network of streets, "I won't take it anymore." It's the absolute fragility of the city that makes for uneasiness, but there is also the very real fear that up to now it was only a joke. Confronted by a serious crisis, in fact, an environmental, social, construction crisis, this city reveals itself untenable. There is an excellent book, that came out a few years ago, *Enduring Innocence,* which explains with extreme clarity the real situation of current construction.[22] Today the business is not to construct but to destroy. The biggest enterprise in the building field is that of the Loizeaux family, or better, of CDI, Controlled Demolition Incorporated, presided over by Mark Loizeaux, and specializing in explosions, or rather quite the opposite, implosions. They operate all over the world and guarantee that faced by the speedy and costly obsolescence of an industrial site, the most convenient thing is to turn it into clear space in a few seconds. Moreover, the same Loizeaux firm organizes demolition spectaculars, especially in Las Vegas, with fireworks displays, *son et lumière,* grandstanding for the public. The trend is that if an hotel or housing tenement is over ten years old, it's ready to be demolished, and this trend is becoming ever more rapid, it could be in six, maybe five years, because the value of the land becomes so appetizing that it renders immaterial the value of the construction. Controlled Demolition Inc. is the world expert in this sector, so much so that there are speculations about whether September 11 could have been an implosion, that the Twin Towers collapsed from the inside and not just from the impact of the aerial attack; that they were worked on by Mark Loizeaux (his CDI is also implicated among others in the seemingly imploded collapse of a building next to the Twin

Towers that had not been touched in any way by the impact of the planes).

New York today is the demolition capital, and has been for a long time—at least since artists like Jean Tinguely and animals like King Kong have been around.

Alexander Kauffman writes in *The Believer*, currently the most intelligent review in America, how the British artist Michael Landy organized in February of 2007, the show H2NY in Manhattan at the Alexander and Bonin Gallery in Chelsea.[23] It dealt with a reprise of the self-destructing machine set in motion by the Swiss artist Tinguely in 1960 in his performance *Homage to New York*. On that occasion Tinguely had destroyed an old piano, an air balloon, bottles, motors, bicycle tires, and trash from the city dump. The destroying machine was programmed to self-destruct at the end. Tinguely had also thought up a machine in a shop window that would destroy the products sold inside the Manhattan store, an evident comment from the militant anarchist on the regime of shopping. The *Homage*, however, disintegrated into a fire that started before the machine had begun to destroy itself. Tinguely therefore called the fire department, who reluctantly intervened over the protests of the crowd. He once recalled that the idea of *Homage to New York* came to him while he was imagining the city before he ever arrived, as he was crossing on the *Queen Elizabeth*.

> With my mind's eye I saw all those skyscrapers, those monstrous buildings, all that impressive accumulation of power and vitality, all that tension, as if they were all living on the edge of a precipice, and it came to me how beautiful it would be to construct a little machine, designed like a Chinese firework, in total anarchy and freedom.

Tinguely said afterwards that he imagined the New York skyscraper as a machine. Michael Landy's performance reevoked the presence of Tinguely in Manhattan, and also an event that Landy himself had staged in 2001 in an empty shop on Oxford

Street in London, where he destroyed 7,227 of his belongings, among them all his clothes, his Saab 900, and works of art by Damien Hirst and Tracey Emin, all in the name of "society's romance with consumerism."

To an anthropological eye, this artistic orgy of destruction might recall the great potlatches of the British Columbian Indians eloquently recorded by Marcel Mauss in his "Essai sur le Don." During their great gatherings the Indians destroyed their belongings to avoid the inequality and social tension that such an accumulation could engender, menacing the continued close ties of the group. Destruction signified elevating the symbolic value of the belongings to a social connective, a little the opposite from the way in which shopping functions today (as a ritual sacrifice of money and of human work to the temporary cult of evanescent individual ownership; individualism defined by the identity of the consumer).

As Kauffman notes, the intuition of Tinguely and of Landy also succeeded in bringing together the spirit of a city and of its inhabitants: two years before Tinguely's exhibition, MOMA, the museum of contemporary art in New York, caught fire and the then director had hailed the event as a grand opportunity to redo every thing from the beginning (in spite of the possibility of losing entire collections, including the works of Monet).

In some way the euphoria has taken on the taste of rust. It is an old modernity with rheumatics that sets in motion the wish for "Destruction, new construction and destruction." The paralysis of Ground Zero and the symbolic aphasia of a collective revision, the recession, the war in Iraq that is costing every American sixteen thousand dollars a year, the world disorder America exports but inevitably reimports, all enlarge the catastrophic scenario well beyond any imaginary esthetic. The speed of dissipation and the fall of illusions with respect to regeneration would make any catastrophic film set in New York—a species that has never stopped nourishing Hollywood—more like an Italian comedy as far as a real alarm is concerned. Finally to transform cities into something modern, using technology, construction, taking measures now and not later, this is perhaps the only task the architects should undertake, provided that they are capable of it and that their competency is not reduced to simple boutique window-dressing.

To be contemporary would signify today taking imminent catastrophes seriously: the slumification of the world, the end of the city through the depletion of resources, the question of survival, of a human cohabitation that takes into account a sustainable environment, with a redistribution of opportunities for access to resources; it would mean adapting ourselves in every way to avoid the entire city's becoming a battlefield torn among ethnicities, forces, gangs, and crazed subjectivity.

The problem is not modernity, but the survival of a glimmer of community in equilibrium with its resources and its landscape, and that glimmer of cocitizenship that needs to be reinvented in this dangerously violent and intolerant present, here as in China, as in Dubai.

> The window: nothing. All right. The void that, from the ground, is called the sky. Intruded by puffy herds and castles of cloud for a while, scribbled across with a fading vapour trail, a chalked rainbow drawn by another plane out of sight. Other times become an enclosing grey-white element without latitude or longitude or substance like blindness descended upon the eyes. Perhaps what I'm saying is that I've half-dozed off, there's an in-between form of consciousness that's not experienced anywhere else but up here. With nothing. The cosy cockpit voice keeps exhorting its charges to sit back and relax. But this state is not relaxation, it's another form of being I have for a while and have never told anyone about. . . . I do not have within me love, sex, wife, children, house and executive office. I do not have a waiting foreign city with international principals and decisions. Why has no artist—not

even the abstractionists—painted this state attainable
only since the invention of passenger aircraft?[24]

I wanted to go away, to get away from all this scrap iron. Tonight,
after buying my ticket today to go back to San Francisco, I was
dreaming of the city through its aromas: San Francisco, which
I had not seen for seven years, is made up of a pungent odor
loaded with oranges and cinnamon, eucalyptus and licorice, of
the damp wood of its houses, of the wind from the Bay . . . It had
never happened to me before: within me I didn't have images
of this city, but emanations, rushes, an untenable sense of being
suspended among barely perceptible presences. A promise of
sensory felicity, the wind that carries fragrances back and forth,
pollen, grains of sand, which links you indissolubly to the soil
and to the mold, to the little pebbles and the puffs of bulrushes.

On the airplane I discovered after many years what it takes
to regain these essences. The plane made me reconsider the
distance between New York and San Francisco, returning me to
suspension, in the void of the skies—once upon a time "friendly,"
now much less safe—of America. The true problem with speed
is that today one no longer occupies space in it. One obstacle
to narrativity is that space has become discrete: in order to fly
from New York to San Francisco one has to ignore everything
that is in the middle, that took the pioneers three hundred days
or more to cross or eighty days for those who preferred to navi-
gate the way around. Today space is fragmented; it's impossible
to consider it a continuous dimension.

The fear engendered in us by cities is the fear of slipping
over the edges, of falling into the cracks, the fear of losing oneself
in no-man's land; between one neighborhood and another;
between one city and another; in the blur between the places
we know and the places that of necessity we have to ignore; in
the time changes we pass through.

In spite of the efforts of artists such as Stalker, we are
blocked by the impossibility of our feet eating up space, and

that is what's eating us: the fear of the grotesque represented by cities today, their borders, their canyons and abysses that open up in the midst of known places, whether they be Parisian banlieues or stretches of sprawl. It's not by chance that a great part of the world is falling into desuetude, into indifference, into being unable to take on the burden of its own upkeep, of human caring. The primary effect of speed is distraction. Some time ago a group of "persons who run" contacted me to ask me to explain to them "why they run." There are ever more people who participate in marathons, who discover them, who run for twenty-four hours in a row, who run for hundreds of miles in places that are beautiful and less beautiful, in parks, on tracks in stadia. They are people who don't do it in a competitive way, to win something— they're ordinary people, at times not even very well trained, who mingle with athletes, with senior citizens and kids, with housewives and retired schoolteachers. Why do they do it? One of them Roberto Weber, has written a book, *Perchè corriamo?* (Why do we run?), in which he seeks to explain himself.[25] He says that it is a question of a rewrite of time on his own body. What effect does running one hundred kilometers have on my body, what is the sense of time that I live during that run, what is the goal, the true distance between the finish-line and the starting gate? It is a distance that varies, because individual time absorbs absolute time. There are people who would never think of doing one hundred kilometers because they have no idea what all that space could be; it is the state of trance that the walk or the run creates that gives that feeling—a kind of hypnosis of the body and of the legs—that becomes space and distance. As if those who run do it as an ascetic mission, to stitch up the sorry fracture of space, a space that no one wants to run anymore, but which everyone wants to transform into schedules and standard travel time.

I believe it was the Californian Indians studied by Vladimir Nabokov's nephew, Peter Nabokov, who ran in a similar fashion,[26] but also the Tarahumara dear to the heart of Artaud following their wooden ball for dozens of miles. The purpose in running

was to remake the time of the world, giving it a pace, to embody
the distances, colonizing them with vision from below, bit by bit,
but continuously, in sequence, as if only the body were the plot,
the narrative thread that could describe the world and its variety.

> The world is blue at its edges and in its depths. This blue
> is the light that got lost. Light at the blue end of the spec-
> trum does not travel the whole distance from the sun to
> us. It disperses among the molecules of the air, it scatters
> in water. Water is colorless, shallow water appears to be
> the color of whatever lies underneath it, but deep water
> is full of this with scattered light, the purer the water the
> deeper the blue. The sky is blue for the same reason, but
> the blue at the horizon, the blue of the land that seems to
> be dissolving into the sky, is a deeper, dreamier, melan-
> choly blue, the blue at the farthest reaches of the places
> where you see for miles, the blue of distance. This light
> that does not touch us, does not travel the whole distance,
> the light that gets lost, gives us the beauty of the world, so
> much of which is in the color blue.[27]

Folsom Street is not far from the Mission District. It is a zone
of warehouses, of huge industrial buildings with giant windows,
which are being converted into architectural offices, cafés, laun-
dromats, and artists' studios. A coin-operated laundry that
opened in a cafeteria called itself Brain Wash, and became the
cornerstone of the revitalization of the zone, with musical events,
benches on the sidewalk, and newspapers and magazines available. Next to the second floor of another warehouse, in a vast
space under the trusses, the office of Public Architecture opened
up. I talk to one of its founders, John Peterson. As his business
card says:

> Public Architecture puts the resources of architecture in
> the service of the public interest. We identify and solve
> practical problems of human interaction in the built

environment and act as a catalyst for public discourse
through education, advocacy [for minorities and the frail]
and the design of public spaces and amenities.

Public Architecture was born some years ago from a manifesto
sent to the studios of all American architects asking that they
donate 1 percent of their worktime to public-use projects. It
kindled enthusiasm, obtaining hundreds of signups all over the
nation, and today it represents itself as an organization that seeks
to transform the profession: the architect should not work solely
on the solicitation of clients, the resolving of questions posed
by the clients. He or she must also be preoccupied with the
problems. For that reason among the first projects of Public
Architecture was a simple structure for day laborers, which
could serve as a rest place and a point of reference for the new
undocumented workforce. Along with this project came those
of constructing housing with recycled materials, of experimental
eco-sustainable housing, transport for the handicapped, projects
for the upgrading of Folsom Street, similar to the Brain Wash
ambience, a redesign of the street to limit automobile traffic,
increasing the use of the sidewalks and the neighboring side
streets, and augmenting the presence of the urban forest. Small,
tangible things. I told John Peterson that all that seemed magnificent, but it appeared to me that he was hoping for too much from
the architects, in the sense that their professional formulation
and the way their studios are organized made it seem unlikely
to find among them the capacity for identifying the problems.
I recounted to him my experience in Renzo Piano's studio and
that of Barcelona Regional with Josep Acebillo, and of the difficulty of making them understand the need for new competen-
cies, sensitivity and different implementations. He agrees. He
told me that knocking at the studios of architects could maybe
lead to big disappointments. Perhaps one should act only on
reforming the professionals, on reeducating the architects themselves, at least until they are capable of bidding farewell to the

kind of architecture they represent today, and imbuing themselves with a true capacity for intervening in a real way, for the
good of the community and the city. We agree that in order to
identify the problems there needs to be a capacity for reading the
contexts, which the architects dismiss as "intuitive" but in fact
are not. It is a question of having a special capacity for "mapping
out" the qualitative aspects of installations and not just the quan-
titative ones, of having an ability to comprehend and represent
the manner in which people will inhabit the space, their vitality,
and their capacity for putting their own spin on their lifestyle.

Still San Francisco gives me hope. The architects whom I
met seem to get it; there was no need to explain to them that
we are on the edge of a precipice—they have already been at
work for years on energy and environmental sustainability, on
the choice of recyclable materials, on the conservation of water,
on the total recycling of solid and liquid waste, on a design that
condescends to heed what already exists and gives space and
power to its inhabitants. Perhaps it's a beginning, perhaps it
really is a pursuable path. The effect that the Bay Area has on me
however is still very subconscious, pervasive. It has something
to do with the possibility of looking at things from a distance,
of breathing in the longing. When I came here the last time,
seven years ago, San Francisco had just been devastated by the
arrival of the dot-com boom, the young turks, unexpectedly
newly rich from the new economy of Silicon Valley and San
Jose. They bought up the bohemian houses in San Francisco,
in the Mission—a zone full of artists, thrift shops, cafés, pubs,
ateliers, typesetters, bookstores—and all of it disappeared in the
course of a few months. Their presence raised prices so much
that wild and creative San Francisco had to pull up stakes and
go elsewhere, to Oakland, or even up north to Portland. This
time instead, the recession, the crash of the New Economy has
brought them back to life—not just the bohemians, but the
Chicanos, the Latin Americans with their music and their tama-
les, the presence of people has returned, of the community who

sing and dance and occupy the sidewalks. My San Francisco that I knew in the 1980s is back. I hope it continues for a while. Last time, in the general sadness I met Rebecca Solnit, who had just written a book on this terrible transformation of her city, *Hollow City,* in which she talks about what happens when an excess of gentrification kills the life that attracted the new buyers, which attracted them but then became uncomfortable because the lively quarters did not correspond to the typical residential quarters, there was uproar, confusion, mingling of different types of people, rogues mixed in with people who fend for themselves, creativity eking out a living. Then I gave her my book *Perdersi* as a present. Today, after seven years, I discovered that she has published *A Field Guide to Getting Lost.* Not knowing if it would bore me or not, I began to read it and there is a chapter that is the most beautiful gift she could have given for losing oneself. It is the first chapter where she talks of "Distant Blue," of the blue of the distance, and then I understand why I am here and why cities, places can become desires, and why only distance can permit them to emerge, an unexpected blooming.

> For many years, I have been moved by the blue at the far edge of what can be seen, that color of horizons, of remote mountain ranges, of anything far away. The color of that distance is the color of an emotion, the color of solitude and of desire, the color of there seen from here, the color of where you are not. And the color of where you can never go. For the blue is not in the place those miles away at the horizon, but in the atmospheric distance between you and the mountains. "Longing," says the poet Robert Hass, "because desire is full of endless distances." Blue is the color of longing for the distances you never arrive in, for the blue world. One soft humid early spring morning driving a winding road on Mount Tamalpais, the 2,500-foot mountain just north of the Golden Gate Bridge, a bend reveals a sudden vision of San Francisco in shades of blue, a city in a

dream, and I was filled with a tremendous yearning to live
in that place of blue hills and blue buildings, though I do
live there, I had just left there after breakfast.

NOTES

1. Orhan Pamuk, *Other Colours: Essays and a Story* (London: Faber & Faber, 2007).
2. Gabriella Lo Ricco, Silvia Micheli, *Lo spettacolo dell'architettura. Profilo dell'architistar,* Bruno Mondadori, Milan 2003
3. Charles Jencks, *Critical Modernism: Where Is Post-Modernism Going?* (Chichester: John Wiley & Sons,, 2007)
4. Saunders, "Accept, Resist or Inflect, Architecture and Contemporary Capitalism," in *The New Architectural Pragmatism*, William Saunders, ed. (Minneapolis: University of Minnesota Press, May 2007) vii.
5. Loretta D'Orsogna, *Il Bronx: storia di un quartiere "malfamato"* (Milan: Bruno Mondadori, 2002).
6. Kim Moody dedicates an entire chapter of his magnificent new book on the Bloomberg era, the era of the triumph of private interests over every public right. Moody, *From Welfare State to Real Estate: Regime Change in New York City, 1974 to the Present* (New York: New Press, 2007).
7. Rebecca Solnit, *A Field Guide to Getting Lost* (New York: Viking, 2005), 105–6.
8. Rebecca Solnit, *Wanderlust. A History of Walking,* Viking, New York 2000; translated into Italian, *Storia del Camminare* (Milan: Bruno Mondadori, 2002).
9. Solnit, *A Field Guide to Getting Lost,* 88–90.
10. Shira P. White and G. Patton Wright, *New Ideas about New Ideas: Insights on Creativity from the World's Leading Innovators* (Cambridge, MA: Perseus Books, 2000) as summarized by Thomas Frank in *Commodification and Spectacle in Architecture*, William Saunders, ed. (Minneapolis: University of Minnesota Press, 2005) 63.
11. A case in point is Fuksas's projected pavilion at Porta Palazzo in Turin. Faced with a request for sliding doors on the part of the merchants for the enjoyment of the crowds frequenting the market, the architect replied that nothing should mar the work of art he had conceived: the doors stay closed. To those who asked that he provide gas pipes for the use of the panoramic restaurant on the second floor he responded that nowadays catering uses electric hotplates, Result: the pavilion was quite useless as far as meeting the need for which it had been commissioned by the Turin Municipality.

12. Elaine S. Hochman, *Architects of Fortune. Mies van der Rohe and the Third Reich* (New York: Fromm International, 1999).

13. Quoted by Hal Foster in "Stocktaking 2004" in *The New Architectural Pragmatism*, William S. Saunders, ed. (Minneapolis: University of Minnesota Press, 2007) 107.

14. *Sketches of Frank Gehry,* film directed by Sydney Pollack, Sony/WNET 2000.

15. Joseph Rykwert, *The Dancing Column: On Order in Architecture* (Cambridge, MA: MIT Press, 1996).

16. William S. Saunders, *The New Architectural Pragmatism* (Minneapolis: University of Minnesota Press).

17. Kevin E. Kelley, "Architecture for Sale(s): An Unabashed Apologia," in *Commodification and Spectacle in Architecture: A Harvard Design Magazine Reader*, William S. Saunders, ed. (Minneapolis: University of Minnesota Press, 2005).

18. Thomas Frank, "Rocking for the Clampdown, Creativity, Corporations and the Crazy Curvilinear Cacophony of the Experience Music Project," in ibid., 26.

19. Rem Koolhaas, "Yesterday, Prada; Tomorrow the World," *New York Times*, June 20, 2002.

20. Michael Sorkin, "Brand Aid; or, the Lexus and the Guggenheim (Further Tales of the Notorious B.I.G.ness)," *Harvard Design Magazine* 17 (Fall 2002–Winter 2003), 30 et seq.

21. John Silber, *Architecture of the Absurd. How "Genius" Disfigured a Practical Art* (New York: Quantuck Lane Press, 2007).

22. Keller Easterling, *Enduring Innocence. Global Architecture and Its Political Masquerades* (Cambridge, MA: MIT Press, 2005).

23. Alexander Kauffman, "'Destruction, New Construction and then again Destruction': European Artists and Architects Agree: What Better Way to Celebrate New York than by Demolition?" *The Believer* 5, no. 9 (November–December 2007).

24. Nadine Gordimer, *Beethoven Was One-Sixteenth Black and Other Stories* (New York: Farrar, Straus and Giroux, 2007) 66.

25. Roberto Weber, *Perché corriamo?* (Turin: Einaudi, 2007).

26. Peter Nabokov, *Indian Running: Native American History and Tradition* (Santa Barbara: Capra Press, 1981).

27. Solnit, *A Field Guide to Getting Lost,* 29 et seq.

CHAPTER 2

Tirana

It is the country where no one ever dies. Fortified by
interminable hours passed at table, quenched by *raki*,
purified by peperoncini with irresistible oily olives, here
bodies reach a robustness that challenges every trial. The
spinal column is made of iron. You can use it as you wish.
Should something break down, it can always be fixed. As
for the heart, it can become fat, kill itself, suffer an attack,
a thrombosis and who knows what else, but it holds up
majestically. We are in Albania, no joking.

—Ornela Vorpsi

SO I DID NOT BECOME AN ARCHITECT. STILL I BELIEVED
that architecture could be shorn of its futility, its lack of analysis,
and its excess of "hubris." Hubris? For example, in commenting on
the debate on the suburbs that had taken place after the riots in the
Paris banlieues, riots that are far from being a fact of the past, but
which still smolder like an ember in the outskirts of the *ville lumière*,
I concluded that if today the question is that the superstars of architecture have taken refuge in the golden world of branding, it was
not like that in the years after the war. That was when the architects
played their trump card as "reformers" of society, as "engineers of
the human soul," as someone might have said, that by means of
constructing the suburbs they were aiming to create the new man,
the citizen worker in a rational and orderly urban surrounding.

In a somewhat pathetic debate in Rome on the Zen district
on the outskirts of Palermo designed by Vittorio Gregotti and

Franco Purini, Purini, who is a courageous person, maintained that he would rebuild the Zen just as it is, because when it was planned, it was based on a social utopia, a "leftist" idea of the Palermitan proletariat, of the repositioning of their way of life, reinterpreted through the *Höfe* Viennese workers. The architects of those years were the legitimate heirs of the same reformative mentality that had founded the profession: experts, on a par with public health specialists, engineers, and administrators, charged with "regulating" the city, with educating the working classes through a new invention: workers' housing. Their role was that of modernizers of a city considered out-of-date, super-annuated, forgotten, denied.

Walter Benjamin, in *Experience and Poverty* in 1933, wrote that with the advent of Le Corbusier and the architecture of glass and cement, the city had forever lost its own "aura," that places were deprived forever of the possibility of being experienced. What houses, squares, and streets signified in the layers of the imagination and collective memory, all the evocations caught in the objects and in the walls, all the things that he, as a Berliner, could conjure up for himself in a "remote corner" such as the Ibiza of that era, all that was condemned without appeal by modern architecture. The assertion by Robert Byron that Le Corbusier was efficient at building henhouses, but not at architecture, is from the same years, and even his sense is in certain aspects close to the words of Benjamin. For Byron, indeed, architecture was still something profound, like hearing the poetry of Rilke, a means of nourishing oneself though walls and streets in a reciprocal sense of belonging.

Probably it is really this history of the professional role of reformative architecture that explains the great change that happened after 1980. Architects were reluctant to become part of an ideology of the disciplinary manipulation of society because they were aware of the failure of ideologies, and of a general professional failure: urban reality, social reality, did not "follow" the disciplinary indications; the English New Towns, like the

French satellite cities, like a good part of the planning and execution of residential modules, had revealed themselves to be failures. Those cities were supposed to change people right away, to reshape their existence into something different and better. A beautiful promise, or rather a fantastic vision, which quickly transformed itself into a real worsening of living conditions. The response, we know, became consistent: negative behavior, vandalism, and social anomie.

Following this general failure came the effect that Jean Baudrillard has called "vertigo," that is, the impression that between architectural discourse and real life discourse there is an irremediable abyss.

The architects remain locked in their vertiginous euphoria, they know that what they do will not have any effect on reality, it will be refuted or transformed in a radical manner. And in the early years, this was the position of Rem Koolhaas himself. Faced with this evidence, the profession closes in on itself, treating its own functions as a purely formal exercise. And this is happening exactly at the time when the entire "modern" city is in crisis and in immense need of being rethought.

In the chapters that follow I will try to relate the ways and means in which I have encountered architecture in the past ten years: in a phase of uncertainty and crisis in the profession, in the moment of explosion in the Paris banlieues, in a situation that made me hopeful in part for a transformation in the practice of planning, which then made me despair anew and decide that perhaps the best thing was for architecture to be considered as an obsolete phase of human thinking.

The account that marks these alternating phases is interesting because it intertwines a little with all the scenarios of contemporary planning: from my involvement as a consultant with Renzo Piano on a project with an impressive social downside for Harlem, the black section of Manhattan; to my invitation to be a consultant for Barcelona Regional, to evaluate and study the impact of an enormous urban project on a vital area of the Catalan city; to the summons to be a member of a jury to decide which would be the most appropriate group to develop and carry out an urban master plan for Tirana. In short, rather a lot for someone who had decided to stay far away from architecture. All of this, however, helped me understand why I was always finding more justifications and external confirmations to account in good part for my refusal to become an architect. But let's go in an orderly fashion. We'll start with Tirana.

Albania, as the brilliant writer Ornela Vorpsi says, is a country "where no one ever dies," in the sense that it seems as though the people are taken by the perennial challenge to the basic rules of good living and cohabitation. Vorpsi talks of the time of Enver Hoxha, but also of the Albania of today, not so far removed from that of yesterday, even if modernized, full of Mercedes and the newly rich. When I found myself in Tirana at the invitation of the mayor Edi Rama, to be part of the jury for the urban master plan, the first thing that I did was to take a walk around as much as possible of this strange center of dust, of anarchical building, cafés under improvised pergolas and climbing vines, remains of old, magnificent Turkish houses, bleak apartment blocks in the Soviet style, devastated nature, elegant Italian mansions from the 1920s, a center in gay multicolored tones chosen by the mayor, a recovered river, a wild and showy shopping center: expensive boutiques cheek by jowl with roast kid stands, model girls and young men with big gold chains and Rolex watches and the assuredness of those who have made their money elsewhere. But there were also the outskirts with hovels, a bidonville[1]—the bidonville of those who at the fall of the regime had believed in the possibility of flight from the misery of the country and of the mountains, who had seen in the capital the hope of social redemption. A complicated city, a good challenge to the intelligence. The jury of which I formed a part was composed of architects, some of them fairly famous, others younger, coming for the most part from Switzerland and Holland. I was the only nonarchitect, the only one on the jury who did not have professional obligations to architecture. The master plan was financed by the World Bank, which was vouching for the transparency of all the proceedings through its representatives. The groups presenting themselves, some very prestigious like MVRDV and Mecanoo, but also others from Switzerland and England, had only to furnish a file showing their competency, and an outline of intent. Edi Rama let us know that according to him, the ones most suitable for the job were Winy Maas and his group MVRDV. During the examination of the files I became aware that, besides a very patchy presentation from MVRDV, there were other less famous groups, less expert in architecture as a formal exercise but more expert in urban administration, who could, in my opinion, really stand up to a complicated city such as Tirana. Moreover, these groups availed themselves of consultants and experts who were not just planners but also historians, sociologists, economists. Following these considerations, I voted for one of these groups, and found myself to be very much in the minority.

MVRDV won. Only the World Bank was cognizant of the fact that I had voted against them and took it as a sign to be reckoned with. And they put the winner in question. I had to come back to Tirana and there the representative of the World Bank told me that it was embarrassing that in every international competition dealing with complex urban situations the tendency was to propose the "architectonical" solution as the expedient. The World Bank, and also the European Union, considered absurd the delay that would be involved in making traditional professional studies, their being convinced that the presence of an archistar sufficed to deal with the most complicated problems. Nevertheless, they also found it absurd that they were frequently constrained to cancel competitions because of the lack of requisite qualifications on the part of the contestants. I can't tell how it all came out, only in outline. MVRDV won again, the World Bank again denied financing, and things are tottering forward for another while.

My experience in Tirana did however give me an unexpected insight: I was not the only one to suspect that architecture was outdated with respect to the contemporary city. The
other thing that I understood, alas, is that architects still carry a
lot of weight; absent true alternative figures of reference they are
able with this weight to provoke a great deal of damage through
ignorance and incompetence, and above all through the strange
conviction that the first thing cities need is an important "signature" that will propel them into the world of fashion.

It's not enough. Because in many cases things go much
worse than in Tirana. The regressions of the superstar architectural style are much more terrifying the more you go to the
suburbs of the world. Pietro Laureano, one of the major world
experts for integrated systems of settlement and resources, was
commissioned by UNESCO as a consultant on the protection
of the magnificent underground architecture of Lalibela, south
of Axum in Ethiopia. He suggested a low-cost solution, using
much manpower, for a meticulous restoration, using mortar
and lime. But the European Union, who were financing the
project, were unhappy: they had a big budget and they wanted
a "name" architect who makes spectacular structures. The job
went to Aldo Aymonino (that is, to the Teprin Studio), who—
without ever even visiting the site—set up a plan of flat, white,
pharaonic roofs on steel pillars, roofs which in short reminded
one of service stations. The first two were constructed, distort-
ing the magnificent sites, hiding the underground architecture
and putting it in major peril, either from the weight of the structure or because the new construction instead of altering the
water course and protecting the underlying architecture, allowed
water in. Pure madness, which rejected the millenary wisdom of
canalization of floods in a semiarid place, a madness which—as
Laureano had demonstrated—cost as much as would have been
needed to feed the whole zone, to raise out of poverty all those
in the surrounding area.[2] But this is still the prevailing logic: a
big architectural signature equals international aid. Once the

disaster had happened, UNESCO after a ten-year time lapse called Laureano back, and he was able to physically block the third construction that was about to be built on an unstable spur of rock. Which is why it seemed to me at this point right and proper to start again getting myself involved in the field where the architects are scratching about. Not just because architecture manifests itself as socially useless, but because it is really extremely dangerous, a craziness peddled for entertainment, a formalism with which to squash the evidence of the necessity of returning to basic needs, to a knowledge of the context and the territory, of the techniques and the traditional manner of preserving resources.

In a 1926 text, *El tamaño de mi speranza* (The measure of my hope)—which the author repudiated because he considered it excessively juvenile, but then was fished up again a few years before his death by some cheeky fans—Jorge Luis Borges described the difference between the outskirts and the *arrabal*, between a world considered simply squalid and the arrabal as a suburb where instead the real mythology of Buenos Aires was created. Borges quoted another author, Rafael Cansinos-Assens, who in a rare work entitled *Los temas literarios y su interpretación* (Literary themes and their interpretation), said that the suburbs lyrically represented "an indeterminate effusion" and described them as "strange and aggressive." Following this line, Borges was able to track down in the suburbs the depth of the Argentinean soul: "We are forgotten by God, our heart espouses no faith, but we believe, oh, yes, in four things: that the pampas be a sanctuary, that the autochthonous inhabitants be very virile, that the crooks be courageous, that the suburbs be sweet and generous."

Because the *arrabales*, the edges of the city that look out onto the pampas—and are the scenario of Evaristo Carriego's exploits—transform themselves into outskirts that were longing for purpose, the keynote implementation of a dream of which the architects were the magnificent standard-bearers. We'll see how the facts turn out.

NOTES

1. Shantytown, usually built of flattened out "*bidons*"—metal containers for liquids.

2. In an article in the July 1998 issue of the *UNESCO Courier,* entitled *Lalibela: les églises sont fatiguées*, Sophie Boukhari sums up this wonderful enterprise: "The result: Europe used up 4.7 million euros of the 200 million earmarked for the development of Ethiopia between 1996 and 2001 to construct what turned out to be some hi-tech roofs."

CHAPTER 3

Banlieue Bleu vs. The Decline of the *Arrabal*

The first discrimination consists of talking about the suburban areas as if they were not part of the city. No sooner is one catastrophic emergency announced when it is replaced by another. One passes from bird flu to swine flu with the same lack of reaction. In 1849, towards the end of his life, Victor Hugo wrote in *Choses Vues*: "What did the Parisians see of all that was happening three kilometers from the center, beyond the inner circle? Whatever was happening, the distance filtered and screened everything." Today we are actually experiencing the death of the street, the loss of contact with the soil, and with the sidewalk, from a superficial and distant viewpoint: that of a helicopter flying over the city, or of a car speeding through on the freeway. We perceive only at a distance, from high up or far away. In this and other ways those in charge display their powers of dissuasion to insure that the people stay home.

—Paul Virilio

STRANGE HOW THE THEME OF THE SUBURBS BECAME THE order of the day in the debate in those years. If it were not for the riots in the Parisian banlieues at the end of 2006, with thousands of cars set on fire, the mobilization of the French security forces, the special laws and the overexposure in the international press, the question would still be languishing somewhere in a drawer. The judgment now, however, seems unanimous: there are few who do not believe that the suburbs constitute a "plague," a nonplace in the contemporary landscape, a gaffe that needs to be corrected. Still it seems a remote possibility: we have accustomed ourselves to the fact that only a part of the inhabitants of a city enjoy the privilege of complete urban quality, while the rest have to give themselves over to coping with the disadvantages of a physically and symbolically marginal situation. The failure of a reformist and utopian effort, which in fact gave birth to subtopia, lurked—and still lurks—behind this commune. And there is another even more absolute failure, that of modern town planning: in spite of all the good intentions of town planners, architects, and administrators to invent pluricentric systems and futuristic agglomerations, the cities of the past sixty years have not changed their scale of values: the center has remained the center and the outskirts remain the frontier that fades away into nothing. It is odd that this start of the millennium shows itself as the most ruthless extirpator of the policies of urban modernity produced from the postwar years until now in both the West and the East, in liberal and capitalistic regimes as much as in state and socialist regimes.

Today the suburban emergency is in reality an emergency for the entire city, an endemic state of crisis. A knowledgeable authority on urban questions, Mike Davis, has commented in a UN Global Report on the question of world slums, maintaining that slums are a widespread type of suburb, more difficult—but not much—to track down in Western Europe, but prevalent all over Africa, Asia, and Latin America, and, regarding neighboring places, in the Balkans and Eastern Europe.[1] Davis records that it was the politics of IMF's dealings with the "third world" that increased the flight from the rural zones, and the future that awaits us is a future of poverty in huge urbanized zones.[2]

The figures of the World Bank and the United Nations are hair-raising. It is said that in twenty years' time 90 percent of poverty will be urban and that 50 percent of humanity will live below the poverty level in conditions of urban degradation.

Subtopia is the new urban situation in African cities, closer to what the Anglo-Saxons describe as "sprawl," that is, a situation of spreading urbanization, which over the years was known as "suburban" and that attracted diverse classes, lower and middle classes, poor and marginal classes, at times together in adjoining urban zones.[3] It is expanding in that way, for example, in one of the biggest and most modern cities in western Africa, Dakar: a center with colonial residences, and then a swarm of one- or two-story villas, for the most part self-constructed, which invade every space from the ocean sands to the savannah with its sparse baobab trees. It is an expansion that is taking place in very critical hygienic conditions and in the absence of any primary and secondary services, but often with a robust network of informal economy and a fabric of clan solidarity, of neighborhood, of ethnicity.

Across Europe

A collection of essays on the *grands ensembles* published by a research group of the University of Paris VIII posed the question of the legitimacy of a comparative overview of the "suburban" phenomenon, of the legitimacy, that is, of a face-off between urban reality in widely-separated countries with very different histories, such as France, South Korea, Italy, Poland, Algeria, and Bulgaria.[4] Certainly this comparative portrayal has its defects of generalization and decontextualization, but it has the merit of bringing out the common characteristics and the spread of parallel tendencies. Moreover, it is actually this comparative approach that brings to light how, in the case of the suburbs, the selfsame modernistic ideology is able to cross not just frontiers and iron curtains but oceans and mountain ranges as well, focusing an intense scrutiny on the question of domiciles. It is interesting to learn, for example, that in France it was the geographers, headed by Pierre George, who first described the suburbs of the "socialist" countries as truly great models to import as the solution for workers' housing. Some scholars on the other hand, have accented the anthropological effects of the existence of the suburbs, a phenomenology of which we as yet know little, but which is already teaching us a lot, whether about the results that an inhuman atmosphere can have on its occupants or about the strategies that could be engaged to render them more accommodating and make them more livable. These are stories from the field with an original flair, much more illustrative than any statistic could be. One goes from the stories of the Moscow suburbs, planned according to a logic of disconcerting uniformity, where the children used to stick a picture of their "babushka," their grandmother, in the window so as to be able to identify their homes and not get lost, to the scenes in Kieslowski's television series *The Decalogue*, set for the most part in the Polish socialist superblocks of the 1960s, to the carefully gathered stories of anthropologist Alessia de Biase interviewing the concierges of the *grands ensembles* of the Courneuve in Paris.[5] From the stories of the *gardiennes* of the Courneuve, for instance, comes the impression of an interweaving of neighborhood relationships superimposed on the anonymity of the architectural form, and the existence of widespread practices of redefinition and redomestication of space in the individual apartments. Some of these episodes reflect the strange and absurd aspect such practices can assume at times. Like the story of a little old guy on the thirteenth floor who had transformed his home into a vegetable garden and a woman on the tenth who had raised a calf, and then found herself with a cow living in the bathroom, scarcely able to turn around.

The suburbs have been the object of "social" interventions, of participatory strategies, of the attention of NGOs and assistance organizations of all types, of the most varied activities of artists and of aggravating media groups—to the point that it's like telling someone that the true centers, the true vitality today can be found only there.[6]

The Effects of Ugliness

It must be said that the liberties taken by the inhabitants with the ugliness and insignificance of the suburbs remove none of the responsibility from those who have pursued this utopia in their own architectural, administrative, or political practice. The crisis in the suburbs today is, on the contrary, marked chiefly by the strident disagreement between the vital intelligence of the inhabitants and the insensitivity to daily life expressed in the plans of the famous and not-so-famous architects and engineers and planners. Above all, it is indefensible that they are still building in the style of the late 1970s, when, as we shall see later in this chapter, the model workers' suburbs all became extinct. A series of French films describes well this discrepancy and the frustration it provokes: it's seen in the harsh film by Mathieu Kassovitz, *Le Haine*, 1995; in *Wesh wesh, qu'est-ce qui se passe?* by Rabah Ameur-Zaïmeche, 2002, about violence, the difficulty of coexistence and drug-dealing; in the magnificent *L'Esquive*, 2003, by the Tunisian-born director Abdellatif Kechiche, where to the tenderness of an affair between adolescents of the banlieues, their interaction told in the tough "banlieuesard" jargon and with reference to their Maghreb backgrounds, there is juxtaposed a school situation that underscores the impossibility of true integration, underlining the marginality of the marginalized. In another way these films are comparable to American films on the problems of the black ghettos, from *Boyz N the Hood* to *Do the Right Thing* by Spike Lee, and have been followed by Italians with films on the Neapolitan and Pugliese suburbs.

In actual fact there is a connection between the way in which the suburbs are made and the ugliness of the social life they provoke. A connection the planners often refuse to admit, as happened during the Italian debate after the riots in the Paris banlieues.

Soon after the conflict, first Stephen Boari and then Vittorio Gregotti reaffirmed in *Sole 24 Ore* that there was no need to attach blame to the planners. The error of the suburbs is a political error; the banlieues rebelled because the inhabitants are excluded from society. The root is political, not architectural. These objections are interesting, but they ignore the fact that the architects have had a fundamental function from the 1950s through the end of the 1980s in making themselves apostles of the suburban solution, that is, of the idea that the housing situation could be "resolved" by the construction of huge apartment blocks in the empty areas outside the city. The format of this type of residence, with its idea of aggregated sociality, is inherited from the phalanstery, but is at the same time a functional concept of "stockpiling" the users in a dormitory space, representing a very precise choice. The city the planners had in mind is a city where the street, with its richness and ambiguity, is replaced by a guided contiguity and by a totally "didactic" idea of public spaces, dancehalls, amphitheatres of reinforced concrete, and kiosks for whatever community service is needed. The ugliness of the suburbs is linked to the ideology of the enclosure of domestic space for the single working-class family, with the reduction of life to a private shadow theatre.[7] There is nothing of the richness found in even the poorest city, where the semipublic and informal spaces, markets, traveling fairs, bars, osterias, cafés, news kiosks, and stalls, all uphold the importance of the street over an Anglo-Saxon pretence of privacy.

From that Anglo-Saxon reformative madness that someone cobbled together, derives the concept of "privacy," and how it is imposed by force and the police on the swarming and irrepressible vitality of the street.[8] In reality "privacy" is the destruction of the concept of a household, of "home" as the center of social and productive convergence.

It is interesting to note how the center of the debate on the suburbs has shifted, as if finally the horror of a concept that negates the city is coming under discussion, a concept of which the suburbs are the perfect materialization. It seems to me that this is also the position of some planners, among them Renzo Piano, judging from the testimony of his recent interviews.

The Suburbs Threaten the Center

It remains difficult, however, to give an overall idea of the problematic issues that actually surround the suburbs of the world and have recently surfaced. The urban phenomenon, which, according to Saskia Sassen, will be the preponderant phenomenon of the next fifty years, has constants that cross continents and countries and that standardize the most diverse geographies. There are, however, characteristic specifics that often go in opposing directions, for example the case of Romania, where urban poverty is pushing a good percentage of families to return to the rural areas, where living costs less. What is certain is that the characteristics that form the basis for the quality of urban living are changing radically, and the new emergencies require different political strategies and plans. The outskirts are a challenge to the contemporary city, reminding those who delude themselves that they can close themselves off inside the walls of the center that the center itself is in danger of vanishing as the suburbs become more threatening. I have already said that one of the major failures of urban practicality in the past sixty years is due to the judgment pronounced on the damages done to the historical centers by modernity and the modern movement in architecture. Suburbs are seen as utopias of the modern city, made up of *grands ensembles*, of skyscrapers immersed in greenery, but in reality they have transformed themselves into nightmares of reinforced concrete superblocks in the void outside the city. From the 1970s on, at least in Europe, the historical centers have been reevaluated and are becoming objects of restoration, wherein is recognized the true city "aura" beyond that of its inestimable monumental patrimony. The tabula rasa to which the Modern Movement in architecture would have liked to reduce historical cities has actually been realized only in the suburbs, places of desolate land and *terrain vague,* menacing areas of conflict within boundaries.

But let's go in an orderly fashion and reconstruct the ways this emergency has finally arrived to knock at our doors, making us understand that we are immersed in the same explosive problems of the suburbs as are Caracas, Bucharest, Casablanca, Dakar, Karachi, or Hyderabad, and it can only be thus because in the shaking-up of the world in which we are living, a good part of the new inhabitants of "our" suburbs actually come from these places.

The Crisis of the Paris Banlieues

The crisis that exploded in France makes it evident that it is not just ordinary citizens, but also those in all walks of life—journalists, architects, administrators, politicians—who are not about to defend the existence of subtopia and that, at most, the admissible debate centers on the way to intervene, and either demolish them or correct their structural defects.

The Paris suburbs, and also those of other French cities such as Lyon, Marseilles, and Montpellier, have become the symbol of a malaise immediately recognized by other countries as something that is smoldering with a more or less suppressed rage, our own marginal quarters included: in Italy it was Romano Prodi who affirmed that sooner or later our suburbs would be ready to erupt, and in Spain, *El Pais* and *La Vanguardia,* two well-read dailies, have conducted a huge debate on the dangerous conditions of the suburbs of Madrid and Barcelona. In reunited Germany, there are over a million empty dwellings, the *Plattenbauten,* socialist installations invented by the GDR or by the Western social democrats to house the working classes.[9] And the situation, with major or minor gravity, is much the same all over the European countries.

Let's start with France. We'll record the facts. It is October 27, 2005. A soccer game has just finished in the Vincent Auriol Park, in the banlieues of Clichy-sous-Bois, east of Paris; a dozen boys decide to take a shortcut to go home. They are young *black-blanc-beur,* as the Paris press defined them, that is, sons and grandsons of immigrants of varying nationalities, but to all intents and purposes French citizens by birth. First of all they cross a construction site. The move alerts the police who send out three squad cars. The boys try to escape. Three of them succeed and hide themselves in an electrical cabin where two of them are immediately electrocuted but the third is miraculously spared. The police were to declare later that they were not chasing them. And it was the rage over these useless deaths, of Zyed Benna, sixteen years old, of Tunisian origins, and Bouna Traoré, fifteen years old, of Malian origins, that triggered the revolt. The contemporaries of the two boys set fire to their own neighborhoods, and *les émeutes* [the riots] continued for over a week. In the night between November 6 and 7 alone, 1,400 vehicles were burned and 395 people were arrested.

Then minister for internal affairs, Nicholas Sarkozy, just a day before the death of the two boys had called the youth of the banlieues *"racaille,"* that is, scum, and responded to the *émeutes* by proclaiming a state of emergency: a curfew with a full mandate for repression by the police. Chirac went on television to appeal to the youth for order, stressing the importance of a new social politics to cure the unrest in the suburbs and to further integration.[10] The international press gave wide coverage to the riots as a sign of the social crisis of which France was the undoubted major vector in Europe. It is interesting to note that in the debate that followed in the French newspapers there was a real disgust for the spotlights of the world being focused on the country—during the week of the fires, both the BBC and CNN were transmitting images of the riots in tandem with the news of the war in Iraq—but in substance there was a great incapacity for dealing with the basic questions. They talked of the crisis in welfare, of the police participation, of the problem of youth integration, and the right wing of the government proclaimed, again through the mouth of Sarkozy, that it was all a question of the problems caused by uncontrolled immigration. In actual fact, the protagonists of this story are French citizens, except they are considered, and they consider themselves, second-class citizens. Two components enter into this symbolization of marginality: one is totally French, and is linked to the guilty and unresolved history of the rapport of France with its ex-colonies and today with francophone Africa. This first component has been aggravated in recent years. The misman-aged exit from Algeria, the political ambiguity in dealings with the Berbers and Algerians who had abandoned their own coun-try by the hundreds of thousands and who recognized France as their motherland, the perilous support for the authoritarian regime in Algeria (and also in Ivory Coast, Senegal, and Tunisia), all this had reached its apex with the admission, at a distance of thirty years, of the responsibility of the Paris government for the slaughter in 1961 of eight hundred demonstrating Algerians, handcuffed and thrown into the Seine.

In order to have an idea of how this distant event was linked to the recent frustrations in the banlieues, one has only to watch Michael Haneke's film *Caché* (2005), which portrays very clearly the emotional state of a French family menaced by strangers who are no longer really strangers but are right here and "living in our midst." The suburbs are the marginal place, but nonetheless very close, where the stranger lives, and—Georg Simmel thought so a century ago—is actually sensed as someone who has stopped being far away and who is becoming ominously close. It is a ques-tion, in short, of suburbs inhabited by the sons and grandsons of immigrants, who have inherited the frustration of their own fathers and grandfathers, and where, in spite of an effective effort at integration, a betterment of their lives has not been the result. In the banlieues, where the presence of youth under the age of twenty often is greater than 50 percent, and unemployment is double what it is in the other urban areas.

From France through Europe

There is however a second, more general component that extends throughout Europe as a whole, and it is the specifi-city of suburban living. The banlieues are discriminant, as Paul Virilio notes, by the mere fact that they exist, that they represent a method of "storage," and that they banish from the center a portion of the population considered less desirable. This is the key to understanding why the adolescents' rage struck out at their own quarter, damaged the cars of the people in their own quarter. It was not just a wish for self-destruction, it was also a desire to physically cancel out the structure that held them away from the true city, those fences and barriers, those towers and squares that symbolize their being "outside." In Paris in particular there is rage against the administrative obstinacy of not wanting to consider as part of the city anything beyond the inner circle where placards are still posted dividing Paris from the rest of the world (as Victor Hugo had noted a century and a half ago), whereas during the past fifty years Paris has extended way past this limit. Paris, one might say, does not readily admit to its growth and considers marginal all those who do not have the privilege of living within the historical *arrondissements.*

One could say that in burning the banlieues the young people were setting up the scene in front of the telecameras of the whole world, for the end of an urban model born out of a utopia that had a huge and efficacious application in France and is still pervasively present, even if shaded with national characteristics, in all of Europe and throughout the world "impacted" by postwar modernization.

There is in the ideology of the *grands ensembles,* in the massive workers' and people's quarters on the outskirts of the city, a conception of society, of the city, and of very specialized housing. This conception at least is common throughout European history as a whole and with which today all of Europe has to come to grips. (The more this conception has been defended at length from the forward-looking unions, wherein the symbol of the workers' objective existence is still identified, the riskier this becomes: in Spain, for example, this is the position of a scholar like Manuel Delgado). It deals with living as a form of social discipline, as Michel Foucault defines it.[11] Housing, a revolutionary expression for defining a place to "stash" the working class, had first and foremost a cultural function, it "informed" the occupants of their status as cogwheels in a more complex system, defining life as a series of separate functions of which the state or the technicians or the planners alone had the sense of the whole. Housing presupposes the end of the "house" as the unity of life and production, and as a symbolic horizon in which to interpose the real networks of primary relationships, family members, friendships, of solidarity and neighborhood. In housing, these networks are dissipated, mainly one sleeps there and one reproduces there like forced labor—the dormitory quarter has arrived—delegating the centrality of life, whether from a Taylorist or a laborist viewpoint, to the workplace, which assumes the prime position, being the hub of the working organization or simply another version of the assembly line.

European Contagion?

Can one talk today of a European contagion spread from the crisis in the Paris suburbs?

One could respond that the flame has not spread, that the wind of discontent and revolt has not crossed the borders of France. But if the inhabitants of the Zen district in Palermo, or those of the Scampia in Naples,[12] or the gypsies of La Mina in Barcelona, have not yet started fires, have not yet given way to spectacular demonstrations, it does not mean that the problem does not exist. Thirty years ago Colin Ward already noted that the systematic vandalism that was targeted against the satellite cities, the English New Towns, products of the most refined architectural research, was not just a gesture on the part of some uncivilized louts, but a precise judgment leveled against the absurdity and abstraction of the urban utopias by the inhabitants assigned to these quarters. A case in point is the model quarter of Thamesmead, vandalized as soon as it was first occupied, just like the analogous districts that appeared as a setting from those years in Kubrick's film *A Clockwork Orange.* The affects of anomie and marginalization have only worsened since then, up until the full-scale and irreversible crisis, of which this example must seem even more grotesque on the old continent, that is, in the place that produced one of the most characteristic European contributions to all of humanity—the great culture of the city.

Today Europe must face the task of redeeming its own suburbs, razing them or else transforming them integrally, reinvesting them with a process of complete resignificance. The problem of subtopia has nothing to do with geographical location. They are different from ordinary suburbs—or from the Borges-style *arrabal*—which could be absorbed in the expansion of the city and become in its turn a new hub of vitality. The history of European cities is a story of the aggregation of villages, of *arrondissements,* of *barrios* and of minor centers into a different kind of entity.

To become part of the city means simply to abandon the logic of knowing one another—all of us in the suburbs—and to enjoy the democratic effect of being able to wander about, to live encountering familiar and unknown faces. Cities are the extraordinary background in which encounters with unknown people and strangers form the basis for being able to invent the future. What is missing from the outskirts is the dignity of the suburbs and the glory of the arrabal; their misfortune is to be the product of an abstract rationality that isolates the dwelling-place from every other function. To remedy the suburbs we have to begin by negating this abstraction. And this can be done by considering the wealth of life stories that have sprung up in spite of everything in these horrible places. Reading this magnificent account by the great Palermitano historian Salvo Licata we hear the richness that filters through from knowing these life stories:

> Paglino obtained the council house in Roccella. His wife is happy with this house and says: "I can call this home!"
>
> Description (which has to be done) of the abrupt trashing of a new quarter: Roccella like all the other cement ghettos, after being taken possession of by the people, all the families of the Vucciria, immediately becomes a wild encampment of aggressive children and

young persons. The steel shutters of the shops are shat-
tered and twisted. The anxiety to reproduce in the new
place all the conditions of the quarter from whence they
came becomes a piercing necessity. "But it was beautiful
in the Vucciria!"

They seek therefore to reproduce the smells, the
sounds, the fumes, the tastes.

The poor of Palermo see the city as the possibility of
an infinite marketplace. And they want to *armare* (open
up shops) everywhere in every which way.

Paglino opens up in Roccella.

Paglino "liberates" a shop front and opens a grocery
store. Actually he is able to put in it only a few poor essen-
tials: bread, pasta, canned food, beer and sauce. A sight
which tugs the heart-strings. In a fortnight the police
come and throw him and everything out in the street.[13]

The Architects' Dream

This radical new living concept that produced subtopia was
carried forward from East to West, unobstructed, by the architectonic vanguard between the two wars.

The so-called Modern Movement in architecture will
assert its own revolutionary role in the words and practice of
Le Corbusier, as well as of Gropius: condemning the old city,
out-of-date and obsolete, with its narrow streets and its irra-
tionality, burdened by its overcomplex and stratified symbols,
and replacing it with the new city, cradle of the new man. The
architects charge themselves with the reform of public housing,
which needs to be rationalized within the forms of architectural
functionality, the principles of hygiene as applied to architecture.

This word of a new city plan and of the importance of the
plan is discussed throughout Europe: men, experiences and
doctrines circulate among an international milieu, where it
mixes with Soviet, Viennese, German, Czech, and American
influences. CIAM, the great International Congresses of Modern

Architecture, provides a forum for this milieu. The myth of the garden city spreads throughout the world in varying forms, in the Berlin *Siedlungen* projected by Gropius, in the *osiedle* of independent Poland between the two wars, which allies cooperativism, urban functionality and research into minimum housing for the people, and in the utopian *Unité d'Habitation di Marsiglia* of Le Corbusier. This wind of transformation will straddle the Second World War and become the watchword of modernization to apply to the whole world, condemning traditional habitat and leading to the construction of a rational and functional society.

Its apogee was in the 1960s and 1970s, but then came the crisis, caused by the total transformation of the whole of society, and, therefore, with the disappearance of the working class, the absurdity of housing that remained solely as a dormitory without a factory to be its altar; up until our day, when the suburbs are tiredly dragging themselves along as the inheritance of a crazy rationalism and functionality.

The *Grands Ensembles*

Let's return to the case of France, an exemplar of this process.

In some sense the Hexagone is a nation of the avant-garde, of avant-garde nationalism applied in a massive and systematic manner to town planning financed with public funds, which in twenty years has completely transformed the landscape of the entire country. From 1953, the year of the *Plan Courant,* until 1973, year of the Guichard circular, which put an end to the *grands ensembles*, France built housing for three hundred thousand people a year, 90 percent of it state-aided. Today one sixth of the national population lives there (one tenth if you discount the quarters defined as "sensitive," those, that is, with the strongest problems of marginality, the most populous and most poverty-stricken suburbs). This enormous endeavor is explained by the situation after the war. The cumulative effects of the disastrous war, the exodus from the countryside, and the increase in population prompted a permanent housing crisis, and justified the mass housing construction made possible by the administration of a program of social engineering.

France has a history of being in the forefront with policies for educating the dangerous working classes in the area of housing; from Jean-Baptiste Godin and the experiments with the Familistère de Guise (1859) to the workers' housing conceived by Henri Sellier in the 1920s and 1930s. The former declared: "not being able to make a palace or a villa for every working family we wanted to put the worker's residence in a block of flats. The *familistère* in effect is nothing more than the social apartment building of the future where comfort is on an equal footing with compliance to the rules of collective living." The latter, Henri Sellier, studied the badly housed from the *catoi* and the temporary housing in the transients' building in the garden city of Suresnes, to see if they were culturally capable of living in collective housing. From its inception accommodation paid for by the state had a reformative function, that is, to teach the lower classes to live in peace and with discipline, to transmit to them the values of urban civilization, even if indirectly, but through the concentration of the work force in apposite containers on the outskirts of the city.

For this operation there will be sanitary, technical, and administrative specialists, in reality all "engineers of the human soul," as the saying goes—and it's the time to remember that it was coined in the East by Stalin.

Subtopia West to East, an Ecumenical Embrace

As a matter of fact it is difficult to distinguish any great difference between the politics of occidental planning and that promulgated in Russia and the countries of the East in the same years from the viewpoint of wartime communism: in the forced march of industrialization, in the five-year plans, and therefore in the control-taking by the apparatchik technicians—indispensable conditions for the realization of a titanic utopia, proclaimed in differing accents from the Atlantic to the Urals.

The modernity allied with the idea of the *grands ensembles* found its inspiring points of reference in the America of skyscrapers, of cloverleaf freeway knots, of supermarkets as well as in the Stakhanovism of the Soviet Union. Housing was thought of and produced as if it were an *infrastructure*. This ambiguous term refers on the one hand to the Marxist vernacular and on the other to public works and their scale, but in any case, underlines its dehumanizing function: the name "infrastructure" tears away from daily life any connotation of voluntary vitality, of eminently social activity. Housing renders passive those housed in it, depriving them of the right to be inhabitants, of their ability to appreciate the lively value of the verb "to live."

The rest is more recent history, but even more ambiguous. The *grands ensembles* so resemble our subtopias of public housing (but in Italy the state has constructed only 6 percent of the existing building properties), the Spanish, Greek, and Portuguese subtopias as well as those of the reunited German and of the Eastern countries after the fall of the Wall—form such enormous homogeneous compact masses, that one has no idea which city one finds oneself in.

Demolition, Future or Present?

Italy was graced from overseas in 1972 with the symbolic image of the explosion of the grand-scale housing projects of Pruitt-Igoe in St. Louis in the United States, constructed in 1955 and designed by Minoru Yamasaki, the same architect who designed the Twin Towers in New York.

After ten years Pruitt-Igoe was 30–40 percent unoccupied, and was destroyed only sixteen years after its construction. The destruction engineer charged with its implosion is Jack Loizeaux, who founded the previously mentioned Controlled Demolition Inc. In 1982 *Le Monde* declared: "We must raze the *grands ensembles*." In Europe the rather timid debate began on what was to be done with subtopias. In France some segments of a banlieue considered to be dangerous, the Courneuve quarter, on the outskirts of Paris, were blown up. The same fate touched others of the Vele, the huge housing project constructed near Naples, in Scampia, after the Irpinia earthquake. The experts were divided. There were those, such as Renzo Piano, who affirmed that a better solution would be to turn subtopias into centers, giving them amenities and public spaces. There were those, like the Swiss architect Lucien Kroll, who set in motion participatory processes in various European suburbs to demonstrate that they were curable by weeding some out of the buildings, by stylized enhancement, along with procedures that would create rapport with the neighborhood and the community. The inhabitants of the "exploded" segments of the Courneuve wept as they watched their dwellings being turned to dust. That same day the television news in France publicly reported a different sentiment: it was hoped that in the future the quarter would provide better living, that is, that there would be better inhabitants.

It is the magic moment of involvement. There are those who maintain that at the end of the day the suburbs are not in themselves a problem, citing as an example an area such as Corviale, near Rome, where the patient work of groups of activists has stirred up the inhabitants' creativity, and discovered that a good occupant could redeem a bad suburb. Franco Purini responds, saying that the responsibility of making an inhuman environment habitable should not be laid upon the people. But in all these discussions it seems to be forgotten that the "structural" reality was already marching towards other horizons.

Today there is demolition; it is its great moment. Controlled Demolition Inc. is working at full strength: with the 1998 fall of the Villa Panamericana and Las Orquideas, two enormous housing projects in Puerto Rico, it has beaten its own record for buildings imploded simultaneously. In 1996 they destroyed twelve buildings in Pohang, South Korea. Throughout the United States from Baltimore to Newark to Detroit, municipal governments have voted to replace the huge multistoried blocks in the outskirts with mixed-income housing, for use by populations of different income levels, at times imploding the buildings before they have thought how to replace them. In 1996 the Chicago municipality predicted the implosion of 15 percent of public housing by 2002. The act of subtraction, of demolition, increases the value of the areas. Obviously, as I have already stressed, Controlled Demolition Inc. is the first to agree, and to describe the implosion (which lasts only thirty seconds) as an extraordinary opportunity to save hundreds of thousands of dollars.

I have already noted that the time it takes a building to become obsolescent is becoming shorter and shorter, and I have already said, and I reiterate, that demolition is the most colossal urban business of the past twenty years. I add only that this type of reality is not so far away from us in Italy. And it is probable that it will be happening before there has been any serious discussion about the future of the European suburbs.

Immigrants Instead of Workers?

Let's again reconsider some of the questions regarding the ideology of the suburbs.

One of the reasons that these have lost their own meaning is that the new inhabitants are a mixed population, which in Europe has much to do with the great demographic changes. As we have seen in the case of France (but the same thing is true in Italian suburbs or, for example, in Spain), it deals with third, second and first generations of immigrants, of a population that is changing the general landscape of our cities and that comes to shake up the zero-population-growth of many European countries, and also to offer their services to the service industry that seems to make up the true future of the European city. These new occupants of subtopia don't do much for it. They live there because they cannot find anything better, squeezing in three or four people to a room, but as soon as they can, they search for a room, maybe more expensive, but closer to the opportunities offered by the center. Their role, in France as elsewhere, is not to replace the vanished factory workers, but to enrich the primary services in the historic centers: shop assistants, dishwashers, twenty-four-hour grocery clerks, waitstaff in bars and restaurants, construction workers on building sites, caregivers, nurses, members of a complicated service industry, the new manpower from whom special qualifications are not required but who take the place of those who are no longer there, the old cobblers, the barbers, the street tailors. They appear as a new component for consumption and tourism, for distribution and retailing. They appear as the new multiethnic landscape of the European city. It is a multitude that invests in small businesses and by its own presence inspires the birth of new activities such as telephone centers, but also kiosks for falafel, chawarma, chicha-brewers, ethnic restaurants, artisan shops, and various activities "of the new ethnic folklore." They are what Alain Tarrius calls the "ants of Europe," poor but mobile and elastic entrepreneurs capable of adapting themselves and inventing new things. And they are essential too in Europe for the growth of supply and demand for a multiethnic tourism: it is they who have saved the historic centers from boutique-ization and from dying of starvation. It is they who have restored the main substance of a vitality that was almost extinguished.

There is no doubt about the need for them in the center. And whether for good or evil no political assistance to immigrants should forget that we are not dealing here with charity housing, but of establishing reasonable conditions so they can continue to do their work, which is also a new service to the population.

This is the new class of workers that constitutes the future of European cities: Berlin, Barcelona, Amsterdam, Madrid, Milan, Paris, London. And now we should be offering them not merely housing but a shop.

Just as in the story of Paglino, what they need is to "armare" a shop. Immigration to Europe is not a clandestine project that the cities have to put up with in spite of it all: it is one of the essential resources that will prevent our centers from dying, from being transformed into shopping centers, closed down after seven in the evening.

Even Paglino, after the destruction of his shop (they should have paid him for it because he was really offering a service to the suburb!) became an immigrant:

> Overcome by the horror of his forced eviction, Paglino went to the Vucciria and got drunk, and then, still drunk, without a word to his relatives, went to the station, got on a train and went away.
>
> In Palermo they wept for him as for one who is dead. They thought at once of one of the "white" eliminations [Mafioso "disappearings"]. Instead Paglino, after three days came back and told them: "The cold woke me up and I realized that the train was in Como station. So I got down, bought myself a bottle of Stock 84 and waited for the return train to come back to Palermo."
>
> Then, mournfully, "See what a fool I am: couldn't I just have bought a bottle of Stock 84 here?"[14]

A Question of Esthetics

This seems to me to be a good point to ask a question: is there something awry in the manner, in the style, in the format of the suburbs, which in short attracts the interest of the formalist superstar architects? It is a banal suspicion that assails anyone who wanders around a suburb today. There is a basic absurdity in the way, in the prosopopoeia, in the expressiveness that manifests itself on the balconies and in the windows, in the obsessive repetition of the modules and the simple-minded ingenuity that seems to hold that one color of a façade or one decorative knick-knack can save everything. The suburbs are constantly being deprecated, from Warsaw to Gallarate, for not believing in themselves, for being consciously attached to their hen-houses, for titivating their own tenements with a flashiness that strikes a false note right away. The problem with the suburbs is their falsity. Every suburb creates itself, even a hideous bidonville has more dignity, that is, it expresses a true human force for living, rather than being a lame utopia imposed by a set of planners on another set of people, whose lifestyle they do not want to share in any way, shape, or form. It deals with a construction conscious of its ugliness, a challenge for millennia to the knowledge of how to build and how to live. I repeat, the inhabitants, left to themselves will end up doing better. That is the now fifty-year-old testimony of those who decided to work with the inhabitants to face with them the question of living.[15]

NOTES

1.   UN-Habitat, *The Challenge of Slums: Global Report on Human Settlements* (London: Earthscan, 2003).

2.   Mike Davis, *Planet of Slums* (London: Verso, 2006).

3.   Mark Clapson, *Suburban Century: Social Change and Urban Growth in England and the USA* (Oxford: Berg, 2003).

4.   Frédéric Dufaux and Annie Fourcaut, *Le Monde des grands ensembles: France, Allemagne, Pologne, Russie, Republique tchèque, Bulgarie, Algérie, Corée du Sud, Iran, Italie, Afrique du Sud* (Paris: Creaphis, 2004).

5.   Alessia de Biase directs the "Laboratoire Architecture/Anthropologie" at L'École Nationale Supérieure d'Architecture de Paris La Villette, and for several years has conducted a careful study of the suburbs of the French city in order to bring to light the life stories at the center of the urban failure of the banlieues.

6.   Michel Agier, *L'invention de la ville: Banlieues, townships, invasions et favelas* (Amsterdam: Editions des Archives Contemporaines, 1999).

7.   Robin Evans, *Il contagio dell'immoralità: casa e familglia nella Londra dell'Ottocento,* in *Le macchine imperfette,* eds. Georges Teyssot and Paolo Morachiello (Rome: Officino, 1980) 268–82.

8.   Taken from the pages entitled "The End of Courtyards in Palermo," from my *Mente locale* (Milan: Elèuthera, 1993).

9.   Mélanie Van Der Hoorn, "Consuming the 'Platte' in East Berlin: The New Popularity of Former GDR Architecture," *Home Cultures* 1, no. 2 (July 2, 2004).

10. Guido Caldiron, *Banlieue: Vita e rivolta nelle periferie della metropoli* (Rome: Manifestolibri, 2005).

11. Michel Foucault, *Domande a Michel Foucault sulla geografia,* in *Microfisica del potere: interventi politici.* (Turin: Einaudi, 1977), 147 et seq.

12. See Maurizio Braucci and Giovanni Zoppoli eds., *Napoli comincia a Scampia.* (Naples: L'Ancora del Mediterraneo, 2005).

13. Salvo Licata, *Il mondo è degli sconosciuti* (Palermo: Sellerio, 2004), 150 et seq.

14. Licata, *Il mondo è degli sconosciuti,* 151

15. These are the observations of John Turner in Peru and then those of Shlomo Angel in Indonesia and Thailand that opened the debate on the necessity of "aid" for the poor in their process of self-construction. The United Nations Human Settlement Program has published a report on this type of practice and on the solutions they offer and the opportunities for NGOs and international aid organizations. See UN-Habitat, *Financing Urban Shelter: Global Report on Human Settlements 2005* (London: Earthscan, 2005).

CHAPTER 4

Crema Catalana

y ventana y ventana y ventana y ventana y ventana
y otra puerta otra puerta otra puerta otra puerta otra puerta
hasta el duro infinito moderno con su infierno de fuego
  cuadrado,
pues la patria de la geometría sustituye a la patria del hombre.

(and window and window and window and window
  and window
and another door another door another door another
  door another door
until the harsh modern infinity with its hell of squared-
  off fire,
and then the country of geometry replaces the country
  of man.)

          —Pablo Neruda

I ARRIVED IN BARCELONA IN 2005 AT THE INVITATION OF Josep Acebillo, who had heard about my eccentric behavior in Tirana. Acebillo was directing, and still directs, Barcelona Regional, the organization charged with major planning for the development of the city. Acebillo had talked to me about the plans for "Sagrera," an area made up of two already-existing workers' quarters with social and symbolic high-density, separated from each other by the valley through which the railway that connects to France passes. The new high-speed AVE service was about to commence, the high-speed train that would link the most important nearby European cities—Barcelona, Paris,

Milan, Lyon, in a matter of hours. Around the construction of a vast new station in which would be concentrated the knot of international, national, and local travelers, Acebillo had come up with the idea of a new neighborhood at the borders of an urban park that would be like a roof covering the railway declivity. An enormous project, in line with the courageous planning that Barcelona needed for its growth and that would require the housing of some hundred thousand people in the quarter. I was very enthusiastic about Barcelona; it seemed to me that finally I had something to do with an architectural practice that was sensitive to the citizens and to their reactions. I recall passing entire afternoons in the little gardens, admiring the simplicity of the urban setting, of the ordinary care and maintenance of the benches, the lights, the little walls, the flower beds—enchanted by the invention of the single bench, on which one could peacefully read the newspaper, marveling at the city culture that did not deny citizens the right to sit and to be seated by the street on the chance that street-people might use the benches. Emiliano Armani, my architect friend, explained to me later that Oriol Bohigas, who decades ago had been the creator of these simple things, had in some ways also been the spiritual father of Josep Acebillo.[1] He had simply decided to see how things were done in France, in Paris, and to learn how to start minimally, infinitesimally. Thus was the new Barcelona born, with money from the Olympics, but with the civic sense of architects like Bohigas who understood that the Catalan city first and foremost was created from the magnificent custom of the people to "pasear" and "quedarse," the custom of debating, eating, walking arm in arm along the street and then stopping, debating, eating, sharing.

Under this mandate major works were coming to fruition: the creation of an immense beach, the restoration of the old center, the reorganization of the traffic pattern and parking system. And into this context the architectural superstars arrived and will continue to arrive, summoned to distribute masterpieces, "marks," "places," to redetermine the skyline of the city: Jean Nouvel with his Agbar Tower; Herzog & de Meuron, with the Forum; Moneo, Toyo Ito, Gregotti, Isozaki, Stark, Gehry, Zaha Hadid, to say nothing of the excellent local architects such as Ferrater, among others.

When I first arrived, however, what fascinated me most was the singular lifestyle, a dense, tranquil, popular sociability, an affectionate and jealous addiction to places, a measure of welcome for the invasion of Erasmus students, foreign residents, tourists, and curious people. Acebillo had charged me with studying the great new Sagrera project and with foreseeing its social impact as much as possible. I started to work in the way that I know best, that is, going around, walking about all day, observing the people, the places frequented and those avoided, the microsocial scene and the transitional scene, the rapport with traffic, the role of the children, of the various age groups (amazed at the crowds in the *granjas* and *cans,* the bars and bistros, at all hours of the day: differing with respect to sex and age, a little according to class, income and origin; whether they are long-term or recent immigrants). I made my rounds with three formidable observers: Piero Zanini, geographer, architect, indefatigable walker, someone who, when a question arises, will sift through the most arcane archives until he finds the answer; Stefano Savona, a film director, anthropologist, archeologist, but most of all, a meticulous observer of the dramas and plots of daily life, of sidewalk activity, of ball games played by kids, of *churros* and *petankas* eaten and relished at strategic points in the neighborhood, and, besides this, an artist, videomaker and photographer, but above all, better than all three of us put together at interviewing people, of making them laugh, of getting them to tell the story of how they came to be living in the area. Sara Donati helped us give the project a third dimension, that of time, talking things over with Peruvian workers and with the Ecuadorian *ecua-volley* players, with the housewives who reminisced about their Andalusian provenance, with the ladies who sipped chocolate at five o'clock in the afternoon. Together we started to understand something. I wrote to Acebillo:

> The verses which Neruda dedicated to his beloved Valparaiso in Chile talk of the difference between the city inhabited by man, where the doors and the windows are a feast of confusion and colors, and the city made by the squared-off fire of geometry, the squared-off city of harsh modernity. These verses could serve as incipit to a work on the Barcelona of the people and the Barcelona of the city planners. The Mediterranean outlook of Barcelona, the grand theatre of sociability and of the changes that have influenced it over the centuries, could conjure up an equilibrium between the lived-in Barcelona and the conceived Barcelona. An equilibrium possible if first of all one concedes dignity to the way in which the people have constructed their own city and their own neighborhood in that minute and intense work that is called living. William Shakespeare also said it many years ago: "What are cities if not people?" A city is first and foremost a large coexistence of a heterogeneous mass of people, part of them—a small part—know one another but the major portion are in fact not acquainted. A conglomeration of houses and apartment buildings, the most beautiful monuments and the best architecture, well-laid-out parks and avenues lined with trees don't make up a city, but are simply the lifeless skeleton. It is the people who give the city its soul, who confer upon it a unique character, filling the streets and the *ramblas* with energy and voices, illuminating the most anonymous apartment buildings and the busiest thoroughfares.
>
> It is also true, however, that the city influences the people who live in it, that the squares, the houses, the streets have an effect upon the way in which the people live, and encounter one another, and that this finishes

up becoming part of the identity of the people, and that often people end up resembling their own city. A great Sicilian writer, Elio Vittorini, wrote in a novel about his country, *Le città del mondo,* that beautiful cities produce "beautiful people," but ugly cities produce dangerously "ugly people." Beautiful streets or ugly architecture, dehumanized enormous blocks or magnificent pathways among monuments are factors that determine whether the lifestyle is good or bad, whether there is outstanding tolerance among people or conflict and tension.

But—there is a but—the inhabitants must be able to invest a lot of energy in their neighborhood or zone to transform a less pleasant place into a world full of life and variety. The patient activity of living is able, with the passing of time, to render habitable even the wildest places and the ugliest of suburbs. In short, to the proceeding statement, concerning the reciprocal influence between city and inhabitants, must always be added the consideration that the inhabitants will manage, in one way or another, with rare exceptions, with more or less effort, to make the place where they live accommodating to themselves.

Barcelona and La Sagrera

This preamble serves to introduce one particular city, that is, Barcelona, and one quarter, one particular district, that of La Sagrera–Sant Andreu and Verneda–Sant Martí and the surrounding area. This rather vast and elongated area will, as we have said, be the object of a grand renovation project. The fast train that connects Barcelona with the rest of Europe will arrive there and this will provide the opportunity to cover the gulch that today divides the two parts of the city, furnishing the inhabitants of Verneda–Sant Martí and La Sagrera–Sant Andreu with a park that will connect what was separated.

First of all, it is interesting to understand how the life of the inhabitants of these neighborhoods, the life that they have developed in the public and semipublic spaces, inside their houses and apartment buildings, in the service areas, schools, gyms, cinemas, markets, cannot only be respected for what it is now, but also for how it will contribute to a positive urban transformation. How will it be possible to maintain and even enrich the social vitality that these quarters have developed, to fill the new projected spaces with significance: the station, the park, the new residences, the framework of the park itself?

To understand how this could happen Sara Donati, Stefano Savona, Piero Zanini, and I wandered around the streets, the corners, the sidewalks, the gardens, the bars, the apartment blocks, all the avenues of this rather vast area of the city for several weeks, meeting people or simply watching them, sharing with them the life and the moments of the neighborhood: from mornings filled with animation and commuters coming and going, to tranquil afternoons, to lively evenings at the shops, of gatherings of children and adults, of strolling along the sidewalks and the boulevards—with the excuse of finding out which are the most-loved places, which are those avoided, what people's preferences are for routes, how they react to distances and to the vicinity and finally how to profit from the opportunities offered by architecture and urbanization or how the one is subject to the other. We chose this type of participatory observation, convinced that along with the involvement of the inhabitants in the decision-making, it would be important that for their part the administrators and the planners understand the context, the habits and the richness of the envisioned spaces, the difficulties and the qualities that people encounter in their own neighborhood. And often there are things that the inhabitants of a place find it hard to express in words. In an interview there are customary silences—things that "seem normal" and even banal but to the eyes of an outside observer turn out to be particularly telling. Outside observers are useful to decipher for people what makes up their everyday life, the way they use the spaces and streets, the entrance ways and gardens. Explaining it to them, we are able to talk about it together and to work out together the outlines on which to build the new pieces of the city.

Barcelona and Its Residents

Barcelona has a very intense history of rapport between its residents and the constructed city, and between its residents and urban development. It is a city with a strong commercial spirit and initiative and that has therefore profited very early on from its geographical position, its favorable climate, and the presence of the sea and a port. The layout of the city, conceived a century and a half ago by city planner Ildefons Cerdà, follows orthogonal guidelines and conforms to a precise grid plan; it has somewhat influenced the character of the people of Barcelona.[2] The city, Cerdà wrote, "is an opening of habitability inset into the great universal road system." Which in practice means that the system that allows a city to be modern, the network of extra-urban streets, which he called "transcendental streets," meets a resistance within the city, in the life of its residents, allowing for the rich interplay of staying and going. And, Cerdà added,

> The private alleys do not form a system independent of the other streets: they allow access to city streets and to the transcendental streets. But if one considers them in themselves, they constitute a link among the buildings which border them. This link, much more restricted than all the others, is, however, much more intimate: it fosters relationships among neighbors, families and individuals. . . . Given that life is a constant state of alternation between repose and movement, living spaces must necessarily open up onto the streets: inasmuch as the transcendental streets do not always offer a smooth and efficacious passageway from the living room to the main thoroughfare, a specific zone develops around the junction where they meet.

In the typical language of the civil engineers of that epoch, Cerdà recognizes that the inhabitants of Barcelona were well up on utilizing the differences among the various types of roadways, and of benefiting themselves from the chamfered "junction" spaces, the actual living spaces of the neighborhood, safeguarding them and putting them in relationship with the great urban mobility. The principal *Rambla*, the Ribera, already existed in his time, and from then on a certain type of "Mediterranean" attitude developed that favored spending time in a public space as a more direct expression of participation in city life.[3] It seemed, and it still seems today, that for all of Europe Barcelona represents a model of that "open-air" life recognized by many countries as one of the more hands-on examples of democracy. It was Rebecca Solnit who defined democracy as being able to walk around among unknown people. And if we think about it for a second, it is actually that, as I have already said, which distinguishes a village, a small town, from an urban neighborhood. To the sense of security afforded by the possibility of meeting one's own friends and acquaintances, one adds the advantage of circulating among other people coming from other parts of the city or even from other cities. The Mediterranean outlook of Barcelona ensures that this sense of security is always mixed with interest in trade and exchanges with other countries and other cultures. A neighborhood functions when the presence of its residents on the street allows for the arrival of passers-by and unknown people without causing a feeling of anonymity. Barcelona is precisely a city that has, in an original and powerful manner, developed the capacity for maintaining its own identity without surrendering a great openness towards the outside. And all this is happening thanks to the fact that its inhabitants prefer being out-of-doors rather than in their homes, and accordingly treat the city itself, with its streets and squares, as if it were a big house.

The "paseo," the being-in, the attachment to one's own quarter, in a city devoted moreover to commerce and exchanges, are a true symbol of Barcelona and today are the key to its international success and to the appeal and fascination that its street life has for the foreigners who come there to visit, and who in recent times, often decide to set themselves up there for more or less long periods. In particular, it is the young European population who have identified Barcelona as the symbol of a way of city living, where the public spaces can be enjoyed and lived-in better than in other places in Europe, a way that is not specifically youthful but which from the outside makes Barcelona seem like a much younger city.

Our District

This Barcelona "lifestyle" is recognizable also in the target zone of the present study and is that much more interesting since the area is off the tourist beat. Even more so, since it is confined among main arterial streets—transcendental streets, Cerdà would have said. In short, while in the old city the layout of the streets and the houses naturally and spontaneously inspires a certain "lifestyle" at walking pace, here in this district where the traffic is much faster and the streets much wider, it seems even more extraordinary that the inhabitants have also carved out a way of life at a relatively slower pace.

This is the first general impression that a wandering pilgrim would have walking around the large enclosure of buildings and squares, streets and open spaces, automobiles and children, promenaders and workers that surround the great gash of the Sagrera, a trip that, to tell you the truth, not too many people take, seeing that this area, up until today, has had its own independent life, but not as part of the larger community. Now it is interesting to reflect on the fact that a project that takes only one name, that of Sagrera, will in the future unite two huge parts of the city that up to now have never dreamed of being thought of as one entity.

The cleft where the railway runs today, straddled here and there with bridges or viaducts or some rudimentary crossovers, has actually separated the two sides of the wound for decades:

from the dense and familiar fabric of Sant Andreu, enclosed
by the megablocks of the Meridiana, from the huge apartment
blocks of the Sagrera, the ramifications of the Clot, and, from
the other side, the scattered cityscape clinging to its slopes, from
Trinitat Vella up to the circular park of the Nus, to the Nodo that
closes the wound; from there to the huge industrial complexes,
some of them abandoned, the long block of the Maquinista, the
orderly shabbiness, the ex *cases barates* of the Bon Pastor, but also
nearby the tall, modest buildings with bars on the ground floor,
and then the massive complexes of the Verneda and Sant Martí,
interrupted by the Ensanche and the vital axis of Guipúzcoa.

It is a huge and varied stroll. But where is this part of
Barcelona going?

Certainly if one goes on foot, by bike, in a car on the two
sides of the wound, the impression is that it takes you out of the
city, that the area nicknamed La Sagrera–Sant Andreu is aligned
along the axis that leads inevitably towards to west, towards
France and the Pyrenees. Here the city seems to lose its central
force. The dense, somewhat restrictive network of little streets
in Sant Andreu interposes itself: it makes you put your feet on
the ground for sure. It seems, however, that here rush dominates, that here Barcelona is in a hurry to be on the move. On the
other hand the fact that the train is already running here, the fact
that fast freeways demarcate the great axis of the Gran Via, and
also Guipúzcoa and the Meridiana, all this makes us think of a
great inclination towards movement and it could be said that it is
exactly this inclination that has prompted the vast multipurposed
station destined for this area. The whole zone will become a vast
area of arrivals and departures, a hub where one expresses the
desire to come to Barcelona, and for the inhabitants, the desire
to depart for other European cities beyond the mountains. La
Sagrera will be the point of the city closest to Paris, to Brussels, to
Marseilles, to Milan, and obviously, little by little, Central Europe.

These are, let's say, the general guidelines and you can feel
them as you walk about the vicinity. The almond-shape that

constitutes the wound and the elongated "s" that constitutes its vital borders glance away, exactly like an almond-shaped eye glancing back out of the corner, looking outwards.

This part of the city, however, succeeds in not moving away; not only that, it creates spaces where the people are, where they stay, and to which they belong. Alongside the impression of something that carries away, there is indeed another: the impression that the inhabitants of the two sides, even with their totally different backgrounds and lack of communication, have become habituated to resisting being carried away and have established very interesting strategies for staying put. This resistance is what produces the "city aura," which allows people to remain contentedly in this zone, to live well here without ever having to go into the center.

And so the dialectic tension between a place subjected to strong traffic flows and the art of building strong consolidations enlivens this part of the city, and says much about its character and that of its inhabitants. And of the possibility that this will become a key zone for all of Barcelona. It is interesting to note that all over Europe the railway stations, as opposed to the airports, generally form part of the urban centrality, even growing with it in density and effect. The stations always produce more or less dense networks of welcome and exchanges around them, which function much better because of their stronger preexistent framework.

What struck me as a wanderer in the Sagrera–Sant Andreu area is the capacity for getting together, the vital force with which people take possession of spaces, and the strategies they pursue to make that end work.

In this chapter I will try to describe, through points equitably distributed in this part of the city, how such strategies assume a spatial aspect, how they form part of the life of the people and of their histories. I would like, in some ways and at least in part, to restore the richness through which the rapport between people and a part of the city is manifested in them; as an infinite series of *vis-à-vis* exchanges unfolds, of neighborhood, of association, of presence, of habits. Let's then speak directly about people and places. I will attempt to do it by telling how the places appeared to me, a foreigner, to my outside view as a nonresident, and then as they appear in the images and words of those who live there and know them over time.

I maintain that there are fundamentally three discoveries made during this investigation. I will only enumerate them, promising to give a better explanation in the course of our exposition.

1) The first discovery is called the "zone of resistance." It is the discovery that the inhabitants of this area are extremely good at thwarting the grand axis of traffic, creating "back" zones, a defensive and domestic retreat where social life is very protected and dense. Almost a popular response to Cerdà.

2) The second discovery is called "minimum spatial definition, maximum social utilization," and it is born from the observation that in all parts of our zone the places that function as gathering points are those to which the architects or the administration have given less-defined functions, squares and plazas, sidewalks, parks, zones of *terrain vague*, abandoned corners. Social life manifests itself exactly where the creativity of the inhabitants is not too encumbered either by the architecture or by the rules.

3) The third is the discovery of the "*rambla* effect," an expression that describes a characteristic common to all of Barcelona but that here reproduces itself independently. It's about the response of the inhabitants to the street as a place of stores and shop windows. Only in Barcelona, and only here on the paseo Puig e Fabra as on Guipúzcoa, do people carry out a special rite, the rite of strolling, which is separate from the rite of consuming. One strolls in the center of the *rambla* and one moves to the sidewalk only when one wants to buy something.

Europe has to recover a certain urban militancy. Paying
for food subsidies is expensive and has to be done every
year. Paying for the cities is also costly, but the cities are
already there: they are not produced yearly. A Europe,
a world seen as a set of nations are slower, with more
opposed languages than a Europe and a world seen as a
system of cities. Cities have no frontiers, no armies, no
Customs, no immigration officials. Cities are places for
invention, for creativity, for freedom.

—Pasqual Maragall (mayor of
Barcelona from 1982 to 1997)

Acebillo received my observations, we spoke about them once, he
answered back that the future he was thinking of for the Sagrera
was a great future, an idea of "cluster," in short a quarter that
would make the rest of the city take off. His was a liberal position,
of democratic government control, as he defined it, strong in the
opinion that Barcelona needs to relaunch itself, expand, become
a "greater Barcelona." I agreed with him and still do, at a distance
of three years, inasmuch as the whole enterprise is exhausting to
get off the ground: the AVE delayed its arrival, engulfed in land
tenancy problems and unhappily embroiled in the worst possible scenario—to pass directly under the Sagrada Familia. But
Acebillo is not responsible for that; and big transportation has
strange logic: these are the same people who sacrificed one of
the most beautiful areas—and one of the most important natural reserves in the metropolitan zone—for the expansion of the
airport. I believe that Acebillo took my observations with a touch
of irony. As a city planner he believes in extensive attention to
lifestyle as heritage "à la de Carlo," Giancarlo de Carlo, with the
same obsession as the great anarchic architect for user-participa-
tion and self-construction. In the meantime I continued to walk
about the Sagrera and Barcelona. The thing that struck me most
is the natural strategy that the inhabitants of these somewhat
marginal neighborhoods know in order to resist being sucked

again into mono-functionality. I sum up this observation with one word: "*jardinets.*" There is a strange system of bars in almost all the neighborhoods in Barcelona, but which, for example in Verneda–Sant Martí, a barrio made up of big, ugly 1970s-era apartment blocks, is more visible than elsewhere. There is a hierarchy of bars and cafés set up so that each block has its own "café jardinet," a basement café where the residents of the building congregate. This intimate socialization spills out into the street, and is even found in the bigger bars, restaurants, and *granjas.* The interesting thing is the puncturing of the private dimension; private life in Barcelona is totally different from Italian private life centered on mamma's cooking, the frying-up of onions and the clatter of plates. Here the mamma goes out to eat at the *café jardinet* and isn't the centerpiece of the family table at home. Eating is a social activity, not a family affair, and this creates a house-street relationship that is quite specific, it even explains why the *rambla* is an equally important factor in all quarters in the suburbs, and why people like to stroll about in their own quarter and not just in the center. This social vitality had become a watchword for me, but slowly I began to understand that it had become something else, a logo, for good luck or bad, of the entire city. A Barcelona whose economic success had taken off based on the offering of conviviality is also a Barcelona that is being sold on the same basis. The idea, an idea of Acebillo and of the new generation of local town planners and architects, is that this city has a special quality of life to offer to the rest of the world, something that it is possible to enjoy only here. The beach, with its teasing and ambiguous character; a liberated and uninhibited city; the principal *rambla* an artery packed with thousands of tourists; shop-window Barcelona, backdrop for big events like Sonar, the great festival of electronic music, drawing seven hundred thousand people in one week, attracting all the young Europeans who are hooked on DJ music: all made possible by the "social standing" of the city, by its social vitality—tolerant, sympathetic, convivial. This model is beginning to show some cracks, however; the blanket of social vitality is not extendable to infinity. For example, it is difficult for it to cover places that are ever more anonymous like Poble Nou, where the hypermodern character of its atmosphere is pointed up and that is now so removed from the youthful, lawless vitality that used to be ensconced there: squatters, artists, gypsies, a place full of studios and underground discos. The Barcelona of these past few years seems hell-bent on destroying the very thing that the young people from around the world come there to find and seems to have overshot the limit beyond which the blanket can be drawn.[4] The symbols of the architectural superstars are not enough, believing in the leap forward to make Barcelona the international capital of informatics is not enough—that leap is not happening. The economic rise was totally constructed on tourist consumption, in a city that with or without the consent of its inhabitants, became the mecca of adolescent Europeans. The impression is that while enjoying economic benefits from it, Barcelona society may turn its back on all that, may start to close in on itself. Barcelona remains a fundamental example for the future of European cities: they attempted here to "sell" Mediterranean sociality and they were successful. Not for nothing did the infamous Richard Florida pass through with his ideas of the "creative class" and "creative cities."[5] But here in Barcelona the creative class is not a Bohemia of artists, experimentalists, musicians, architects, or graphic artists—it was that once, yes, but it faded away after a few years. The real creativity was in the attitude of the people, of the poorer classes and the middle classes, a magnificent attitude, magnificently fragile. Once the city discovered that it had a problem with public order, that it had to impose strict rules for the discipline of the streets, it then began to kill all this. A city that was an interesting interplay of foreigners and locals, of established customs and intrusions, had condemned itself in favor of a sugared-up version for tourist consumerism.

The Barcelona of today is schizophrenic: it functions like a meat-grinder of tourists in the *case antiq* and as a haven for tourists in the nineteenth-century part of the *manzanas* of Cerdà. There has been no wedding between the two spheres and, above all, that international creative class that intoxicated Florida has not been created. "Creative Cities" is a marketing concept that has already run its course. Cities become creative if first of all they maintain an equilibrium between everyday living and the inrush of the foreign, between the home front and the welcome wagon. If this conviviality becomes transmuted into a brand, one immediately has falsification, which can, let us carefully note, also be efficacious on the commercial plane but at a certain point will sap the energy from the entire social and city life. Today Barcelona is at a rather complicated crossroads. The revolution that the architects have achieved there has been absorbed by the branding to which the same architects and administrators have given too much credit. If your city transforms itself into a logo, sooner or later it is better if you go and live somewhere else. The street, however, remains interesting, and nowhere is it said that one can't invent a different method; there is a profound idea of city culture as a real European heritage, and this has worked. The disaster is in applying the model system of the fashion trade, to which the architects today are the testimonial. When does an architectonic masterpiece become an "excess," "too much," so that the city can no longer put up with it? And is it possible that the city planning model should still aspire to be the "scoop," the leap, the scandal, the total invention, the tabula rasa of what was there before? These are questions that Barcelona would do well to ask itself because its position in the vanguard in Europe could cost it a fall exactly on the scale of the livability that launched it on the market. At the end of the day Barcelona is a model of the gentrification of an entire city that was as attractive as a great Trastevere, as a great Montparnasse, and, once she had attracted the crowds, she found herself deprived of the costume with which to do her striptease.

> The key expression [in Catalan] of xenophobia is violently loaded: *xarnego*. Originally, *xarnego* was fairly neutral and

meant a Catalan whose parents had come from different valleys. Then it shifted to "foreigner"; a peasant living
in one valley of the Ampurdan, for instance, would use
it of a peasant from the other side of the hill. But with
immigration, it came to denote—in the most pejorative
sense—any working-class person of non-Catalan Spanish
origin living in Catalunya. Today it has the same power of
insult as "nigger" does in America.

—*Robert Hughes*

Obviously there is another element to be taken into consideration as to why cosmopolitan Barcelona has transformed herself
into a simple Crema Catalana.

Behind Acebillo's dream, that of an expanding city that
would become "greater Barcelona," a city of two million inhabitants, was the more or less acknowledged model that the enthusiasm of the avant-garde Catalan architects had dragged out after
the fall of Francoism.[6] The Catalanism of people like Bohigas
was for Catalonia to have a European leaning, a cosmopolitan
capital as the counterpoint of Paris rather than of Madrid. Once
Franco had fallen, the opportunity provided by the Olympics,
together with the economic boom linked to a liberalization of
the markets and an unscrupulous use of real estate, launched
Barcelona on a truly European circuit. The city was filled with
foreigners, and as we know, became the preferred destination for
Erasmus students and the youth of Europe. Over a ten-year span
this phase of enthusiasm has slowly given place to a dearth of
ideas, to an advanced crisis that presented a transformed city to
the new generation of planners but without managing to transmit to them the cosmopolitan dream. The gentrified Barcelona,
which certainly represented an optimal opportunity for the tourist industry, lacked a more profound discourse of tolerance and
openness: as long as the foreigner was a tourist this was all right,
but for a city composed of both foreigners and locals, a broader
and more general dream was needed. The impression is that

a totally technical approach had taken over—an efficient city, disciplined, with a police force visible everywhere, in short, a more technically developed city but without a soul with which to inspire itself. Thus the triangle imagined by Acebillo, an ideal continuation of Cerdà's network, a triangle that had as its strong points the Sagrera, the real estate use of Poble Nou, and Project 22@Barcelona, basically unites places with nothing in common, that no longer form a texture of affiliation, of vital Catalan sociality; they are no longer the places of an undisciplined Bohemia that utilized abandoned spaces and ex-factories and they are not the neighborhoods envisioned for the arrival of an international middle class of artists, creative people, informatics operators. The foreigners came and went, because the city had not changed its attitude towards the long-time resident foreigner. The dream of the anti-Franco aristocratic avant-garde, dissipated in an architectonic technicality, and had to come to grips with a nationalism that in recent times increasingly assumes the characteristics of an anti-European shut-down—the city is rolling itself up like a hedgehog in a repetitive amalgam of autonomous slogans whose only effect seems to be the strangulation of its international inclination. With this in mind, it is ironic that the shut-down is linguistic, the necessity of learning Catalan as a condition for becoming part of the workforce, when it was actually Castilian that illuminated for the European and American creative classes the idea that Barcelona was an open, accessible place, to breathe in and interact in. Today there are no ideas, and the saddest thing is that the city doesn't even have an architectonic memory capable of reminding itself that it was an international place for entire generations of Latin American writers, poets, and artists. The anti-Castilian hatred is on a par with the stinginess towards those who have given so much to this city by their presence, such as García Márquez, Vargas Llosa, Bolaño, and many, many others. For example, no one has thought of competing with Paris and its Maison du Monde Arabe, with a great House of the Americas that could become an architectural symbol of internationalism. Durruti is dead once more, and Barcelona's aptitude as a symbol of liberty seems to have been subsumed into the Barça soccer league. Certainly this coincides with the end of an intellectual vocation for Catalan architects. Their lifespan is brief, and they content themselves today with being recognized as exponents of a school of form rather than as provokers of new subject-matters. A pity, for a city that really had powerful architects for at least twenty years. But perhaps powerful architects are worse than powerful philosophers; at a certain point they lose themselves in their heavenly kingdom.

NOTES

1. A history of the way architects seized power in Barcelona at the fall of Francoism, the way they trained, and the rapport between the generations of architects can be found in *La ciudad de los arquitectos* by Llàtzer Moix (Barcelona: Editorial Anagrama, 1994). One should also look at the first chapter of Robert Hughes's magnificent book *Barcelona* (New York: Alfred A. Knopf, 1992), entitled "The Color of a Dog Running Away," which tells with gusto of the years of Barcelona's invention by its architects.

2. Ildefons Cerdà, *La théorie générale de l'urbanisation* (1867), Antonio Lopez de Aberasturi, ed (Paris: Éditions de l'imprimeur, 2005).

3. Manuel Arranz, *La Rambla de Barcelona. Estudi d'historia urbana* (Barcelona: Raphael Dalmau, 2003).

4. For a review of the model Barcelona that is different from mine and for me a little too closely linked to a Meccano-Marxist reading, one should see the nonetheless invaluable work of Manuel Delgado, *Elogi del Vianant: del "model Barcelona" a la Barcelona Real* (Barcelona: Edicions de 1984, 2005).

5. Richard L. Florida, *Cities and the Creative Class* (New York: Routledge, 2005).

6. Peter G. Rowe, *Building Barcelona: A Second Renaixença* (Barcelona: Barcelona Regional Actar, 2006).

CHAPTER 5

Architecture Washes Whiter

WHAT HAPPENS WHEN A HIGHLY TALENTED ARCHITECT, a powerful client and a popular neighborhood come together? What happens is that things become a little complicated, especially if the architect is Renzo Piano, the client is Columbia, one of the biggest (and one of the whitest) universities in New York, and the Manhattan neighborhood is Harlem. Whoever sees contemporary architecture as an interaction of volume and models and of show-performances might think that once a beautiful form has been invented and approved by the client, the rest would be an interplay of images and style. In reality, architecture, above all if it is dealing with a huge transformation, always has a social impact, and creates a force-field where actions and reactions have consequences over time. From the enlightened and progressive new president, Lee Bollinger, Renzo Piano received the responsibility for designing the General Plan and part of the buildings that would comprise the new campus to the north of the old Columbia. Which means thinking of the development of an area that extends for ten blocks, from 125th Street to 135th Street, bordered by Broadway on one side and on the other the river that divides New York from New Jersey. It consists of black Harlem, the neighborhood that is home to the Black Panthers, the Apollo Theatre, the Cotton Club, and the films of Spike Lee.

The area will have to house twenty-five thousand new students. The plan foresees the construction of an entire campus with facilities for research and teaching, with services and connections with the rest of the city. The new president selected Piano because he knows that the pathway is strewn with thorns. Indeed, Columbia has a bad reputation for the way it has behaved in its dealings with the inhabitants of the adjacent neighborhood and with those of Harlem. Furthermore, everyone knows that Columbia is the third-largest real estate mogul in the city: it owns areas, buildings, apartments, and for some time has wanted to expand to the north where it has acquired real estate and lots in great quantity, profiting from the general amelioration of life in Harlem, where the crime rate plummeted dramatically during the Giuliani years. Clinton established his offices in the neighborhood, and a portion of the black middle class invests there and lives there. But Harlem is also a poor area, where living below the poverty level is the norm and the literacy rate is extremely low. Besides which it is the area most symbolic of the life and the tormented history of blacks in America. Malcolm X, who explosively led the revolt against racial segregation and then against Columbia because of a series of real estate acquisitions of public spaces that amounted to an attempt to corner the market, was killed here.

Having said all this, what could someone like Piano do? Instead of falling into line and choosing a more tranquil field, say, a beautiful little masterpiece of a museum in some city whose image is in need of redemption, or a fire station transformed into an artistic sculpture, he accepted. However, given that he has enormous talent, he worries. He wants the project to be something that is not "against" Harlem, but rather an opportunity to give the area public spaces, theaters, an art academy, recording studios for the local bands, galleries open to musicians and other local artists, a grand plaza accessible to everyone in the center of the campus. In short, he wants a shotgun marriage between Columbia and Harlem, and that they accept the consequences of their promiscuity. And he comes up with a very ambitious plan, which first of all challenges the New York predilection for building the greatest quantity of cubic meters. Instead, he streamlines, lowering the heights, anticipating that the first two floors that give onto the street will be shops and public spaces. He wants the campus to be accessible and permeable where one can breathe the tough but exciting air of the "other America."

The technical services, the laboratories, the facilities for the University, will be underground, carved out of the hard Manhattan rock, and the rest of the buildings will rise twenty or so feet over them. Besides that, the whole must meld with the architecture of this zone that overlooks the river, with its characteristic buildings and iron constructions from the early part of the twentieth century, the great arches that support the railway and the elevated subway.

Not content with that, Piano also wants to understand what is happening in the quarter and how the neighborhood itself is reacting to the initiative. He asks Columbia for maximum transparency and communication, and knowing that in such a complex place the word "participation" is difficult to articulate, he seeks other professional experience. He asks me, as an anthropologist, to give him a hand. Thus once more I am walking around, talking to the people; I live in the neighborhood, I contact the leaders and those who suspect that Columbia is only a huge building speculator who will chase away the traditional inhabitants in order to invent for themselves a trumped-up quarter that has nothing to do with the America of jazz, of the rights of minorities (the Spanish are intimately mixed in with the blacks here), and hip-hop. Columbia is not very pleased that the Genoese architect is worrying about the impact of the project (how many people to chase out, how to raise the rents?), but Piano refuses to believe that his sole responsibility is to the University. Here he is playing the game of reinterpreting the neighborhood north of New York to which the actual inhabitants are essential. He understands, perhaps he has always known, that architecture has an enormous civic responsibility and that this project is either sensitive to its context or it is better not done. He knows that he has to be able to confront an extremely powerful client while representing the interests of the community. He does it with great professionalism, but he is redefining a vocation that too many of his colleagues treat with disenchanted disengagement. He takes risks, he gets mad, he threatens to quit, he obtains results, he listens. It amazes me that such a man, so decisive and at the same time so modest, can hone in on the essential truth at the core of the project instead of merely recording it on his drawing board.

The neighborhood is lively, full of people who to be sure would like to see improved services and the defeat of degradation, but who are clinging to the incredibly symbolic force of the place. Harlem, it has to be said, is one of the few neighborhoods filled with open spaces, with wind and sun, with red-brick houses and residential streets with a human aspect. Here the new look launched by Jennifer Lopez combines with barbecues on the sidewalks, the street life of the Latinos, the rhythm of blasters, the sneakers laced together and thrown over the power lines. Here blacks still have their own activities; they are capable of stirring things up in ways not usually encountered in Manhattan.

One sunny Saturday on 125th I saw a beautiful, black forty-year-old woman pushing a baby carriage with a little boy go into a very trendy Chicano fashion store. The manager, white and pomaded, said to her: "Welcome, here you'll find what you're looking for," and she, without missing a beat, pointing her finger at him like an Eminem video, said: "I want you, baby!" It's a Saturday, and in the crowded subway—Harlem is enviably linked to downtown by a few stops—a black girl, surrounded by five kids, is dressed in a *very* risqué top, braless, and big, *very* low-slung pants. To the comments of the bystanders she responds with a pride that is far removed from politically correct American Puritanism. She has the right to be seminude and others can put up with it. Only two stops further on, at 104th, where Columbia University is today, one sees only well-dressed Britney Spears types with their badges giving them access to the well-supervised gates of the campus firmly pinned on.

Still it is also in this institution that the wish to change was born. There are professors like Peter Marcuse, son of Herbert, he of *The One-Dimensional Man* and the revolt at Berkeley, who worked on behalf of the inhabitants; or students such as the congenial filmmaker Leah Yanatos, who as her graduation thesis made a video of the protests by the inhabitants of Harlem against the redevelopment project.

I went around the neighborhood with Leah, who knows very well how to interview children: it's Sunday, they're playing baseball and talking in their homes, of how much they love Harlem, in spite of the pushers that are still hanging around, the drive-by shootings and the sanitary conditions in the big apartment buildings, which leave much to be desired.

"What do you think of the fact that Columbia is coming here?"

"Great, great," they reply, "we can challenge their baseball team!"

I also wander around at random a bit with Piano then, and he will point out to me the places that he likes, diners, the piano repository, the train trestles, the historic buildings, and I will try to tell him about the thing I discovered in the latest hip-hop complex, of the shop for extra extra large sweaters and of the incredible Latino bakery where the wedding cakes have mixed couples on the top. We both know that this enterprise will take a long time. The plan will be developed over the next thirty years. We also know that it will involve an increasingly edgy public discussion with local committees, dedicated intellectuals and tenants' organizations. One of the most critical groups is headed by a whiz-kid geographer, a professor at Johns Hopkins University, Neil Smith, who has founded an association called The Center for Place, Culture and Politics, which has declared itself very skeptical about Columbia's real intentions in opening itself up to the community. The difficulty for Renzo Piano will be to get those responsible for such a great endeavor to understand the importance of keeping an open dialogue between the two sides. It is a new logic. We will have to make those at Columbia understand that they are, however, formidable opponents. It is difficult to think that an architect to whom such a responsibility has been entrusted can willingly align himself with the context that could bring the project down. But this also signifies having talent and being among the great professionals: giving dignity to architecture and an independence from the commitment to the slavery of the marketplace to which architects, even great ones, have too often easily acquiesced.

Dear Renzo,

Some years have passed since I wrote this article for *La Repubblica delle Donne* and since you received the commission from Columbia. I have to confess that there have been moments when I have had doubts about my not becoming an architect, and they have been when I watched you at work. It seemed to me that your approach was so deft and at the same time so sharp, that the idea of being able really to transform the world by replanning it fascinated me. In Paris, at your studio on the Rue des Archives, museums, hospitals, skyscrapers, newspaper publishing houses, city sections were taking form and it was impressive to see how space could be molded though the corrections you made with your drawing pen, passing inspection on the projects in formulation. Thus when the campus for Columbia began to take shape under your rapid-fire intuition, the entire surrounding neighborhood seemed to take on life, your intention being to take the opportunity to enrich the social life of Harlem and not to destroy it. I had already told you that it seemed important to me to impress on Columbia a philosophy in which the ground floor, the *rez-de-chaussée*, is open to the community, offering museums of Latin pride, recording studios for the local hip-hop, libraries for the history of the neighborhood, spaces for children. And you had created a magnificent image of a transparent, accessible campus that would provide the neighborhood with a connection to the new arrivals, an opportunity for public space, and spaces for inventing. The size and the shape of the big central plaza is reminiscent of Siena's Piazza del Campo and is, as that is, the focal point of a neighborhood seeking not gentrification but social redefinition. Once I accompanied you to New York, and on that occasion you had already reacted to Columbia's wish that you set aside your observations and preoccupations for the life of the neighborhood; you were angered by the pettiness of the approach of your client, who suggested that you mind your own business, and, in short, do your job as an architect.

On that occasion I had met with the first bastions of the neighborhood committees who were demonstrating their own perplexity and denouncing Columbia's project to "clean up" Harlem of its historic but inconvenient appearance. Things evolved in a strange, but very obvious manner. Columbia had begun to take over, had begun to pay people to go away, to push local enterprises—offices, small businesses, shops—to move out. Black or Hispanic Harlem with its very public look, a little run-down and a little gimcrack, its street life, its music, its characters, all that didn't fit in with the future. The neighborhood was going to be laundered, because it had to become objectively whiter, ready to recycle itself in the great Manhattan real estate market. Then it seems to me that they began to take away more and more space from you: the main square was no longer under your competence, neither was the layout of the entire campus; the cubic space that you wanted to limit was expanded to cover the lots, while the mayor of New York was reaching out to the real estate ambitions of Columbia, extending the building limits. A large part of the project was entrusted to SOM, to the infamous Skidmore, Owings, and Merrill, the most obedient planners in the city's real estate market. You were left with one corner of the campus, the one closest to train and subway access, a fascinating corner, between Broadway and 125th, which at the beginning was considered for the art department, its sailboat imagery a symbol of the lightness of the knowledge that was going to be imparted there. Then even this destination was changed, and the buildings acquired a fuller, more padded aspect, following the exigencies of a client increasingly lacking in poetry. The last time you spoke to me about the project you were very disheartened because your last visit had been fraught with a polemical confrontation with representatives from the organizations, community boards and groups who were resisting the Columbia project. Columbia conducted itself as usual, that is, badly, paying off local administrators and citizens in order to pass everything they wanted, refusing to take into consideration their observations, their questions, their perplexity, including many very powerful aspects, such as, for example those having to do with the deep "bathtub" to be constructed underground, destined for biotechnological experiments and research into pathogenic agents such as SARS, anthrax, smallpox, typhoid, and bird flu.

These groups have presented one of their own plans, controversial and in many ways counteropposed to Columbia's unique, powerful plan. Columbia through its authoritative mouthpiece have always proclaimed to be doing good for the area, bringing in innovation, technology, civilization, work. They have opened various employment offices in Harlem to offer qualified workers jobs inside the campus, knowing full well that few of the inhabitants of the neighborhood have the requisite qualifications for the work. And above all they have not even vaguely taken into account the symbolic aspect of Harlem, of its being symbolic of the presence of African-Americans in U.S. territory, the setting for a long, sad history, a history made up of many Harlem Renaissances, and much more. No, for Columbia it is only a question of laundry, of rendering the neighborhood as white as possible, sweeter, more polite. A project that could be shareable, if the history of a place meant something: it's as if Columbia suddenly decided to install itself in Rome's Trastevere and to transform it into a shopping mall among the beautiful typical little houses. Furthermore, dear Renzo, I believe they have used you to present an important name, the face of a sensitive person who is renowned for his thoroughness, a face with which to cover up their own total reluctance to participate in a dialogue. Because of this all your meetings with the local community have made you a target of contention. All this is very sad, because obviously it was not your intention to cover up for Columbia's total lack of sensitivity. Today the situation is even more grave.

The Coalition to Preserve Community, coordinated by Tom DeMott, another intellectual working alongside Peter Marcuse and Saskia Sassen, on December 10, 2007, presented a community opposition document to the Columbia project:

> The Columbia plan does not include affordable housing, nor does it include regulation to oblige each construction company working in the area to provide low-cost housing for residents. Instead, the plan calls for the eviction of 132 families from the neighborhood and for the evacuation of some 5,000 residents, according to prudent estimates by Columbia University. Here is a community with its own history, with residents and activities that have been in existence for more than fifty years: mechanics' workshops, artists, furniture makers, restaurant owners. Columbia could provide for mixed development which would protect what already exists, but things are going very differently, with Columbia on the one hand continuing to offer packets of money to send them away from there, and on the other hand touting campaigns of so-called community coalitions against drugs. A chemical bathtub on three underground levels should not be constructed in a densely populated area and in a zone subject to seismic activity. The thermoelectric cogeneration plans, together with the vast projected underground excavations, will provoke huge earth tremors, making necessary the interruption of sewer systems and electrical conduits and the closure of streets for many years, with an increase in the inconveniences and environmental inequities facing the resident population. In addition, access to the waterfront

will be curtailed for many years. The public space at the
center of the project (mandated by law) will be used as a
recreation space by the University, and not as a resource
for the whole community. Three historic buildings will
be razed, and the historic conservation of the quarter is
being ignored altogether. Most important of all, one of
the most composite and diverse communities in New
York will be inexorably erased.[1]

Dear Renzo, it's probable that there is little to be done, things are
moving forward, and Columbia is a giant, a Goliath; every coalition that confronts it is a mini-David and we don't even know
if they have a good sling. Your part in the project is so limited
that you certainly are not responsible for the laundering of the
neighborhood. What bothers me is that Columbia has used you
for a normal clean-up operation. I think that for the good of the
profession and for your own prestige, it would have been better,
and indeed would be better, I'll say it in the present, for you
to disengage yourself strongly from the heavy, unpleasant and
disgusting Columbia procedure. I don't think you need them,
rather the testimony of an architect who denounces the pettiness
of such a big client could only help establish a more transparent and democratic process. But it is not up to me to teach you
a commitment you have already demonstrated in many other
situations. What worries me here, however, is observing how
all this impinges on the limitations of the architectural profession. As the people from the World Bank said to me in Tirana:
why don't architects equip themselves differently? Why when
confronted by a client who is requesting a socially disruptive
intervention do they not offer the whole gamut of their competency, precisely to avoid the clients saying to them: the social
aspect is our affair, you get on with the architecture? Today it
is to be hoped that all the know-how of environmental impact
assessment, of ambient impact, becomes advocated by planners,

just as it is to be hoped that the value of social impact assessment will also be advocated.

If we don't want to hear the swan song of architecture, with the work of a handful of the last great workers supplanted by the logic of real estate excuses, it seems to me essential that the profession as a whole must change. Instead of seeking out random projects, they must truly become planners of the quality of life and of living. If this is utopia, or if one thinks it to be, I can only be happy about it. What is certain is that times have truly changed. Talking to Kenneth Frampton, who, as you know, holds you in high esteem, it came out that if architects really want to enter into the changing times they have to become more intransigent and more complete, they have to consider the city as a whole. This may seem ingenuous, but in reality we have arrived at a situation where the simple things need to be recovered, such as, for example, the choice between a community that makes a livable and habitable neighborhood and a white-washed quarter for disciplined inhabitants and their bodyguards. Passing through West Harlem recently, on the streets parallel to 125th today illuminated and redone, I saw the little red-brick houses, each with its wide front stoop, the swept sidewalk, and lots of For Sale signs—I had in my head echoes of the recession and the mortgage crisis—and I thought that for sure one could finally enjoy all the beauty of this neighborhood, appreciate its qualities . . . what a shame that what is coming here is not so very different from the embalmment of which all of Manhattan is becoming the symbol, a Disneyland of shopping, a Disneyland in which, as opposed to the rest of the world, everyone is white, everyone speaks English and has a sturdy gate to keep out the rest of America, of which 40 percent speak Spanish, who vote for a black man, who want to liberate themselves from the ghosts of these past horrible years.

NOTES

1.   www.stopcolumbia.org and www.columbia.edu/cu/cssn/expansion

CHAPTER 6

Italian Cities, C & G (Cool & Garbage)

Once we visualize cars as chips with wheels, it's easier to imagine airplanes as chips with wings, farms as chips with soil, houses as chips with inhabitants. Yes, they will have mass, but that mass will be subjugated by the overwhelming amount of knowledge and information flowing through it. In economic terms, these objects will behave as if they had no mass at all. In that way, they migrate to the network economy.

—Kevin Kelly[1]

Palermo is cool.

—Slogan from the Publicis campaign for promoting the Commune of Palermo, 2007

MY CITY IS IN THE HANDS OF THE BANDITS. THIS IS THE refrain that runs through my head every time I return to Palermo. What reason do I have for thinking this? I could reply: fifty years of life experience here and in other places and then having the good fortune of being able to see the outside view and not just the blighted "realist" view from inside. The truth, however, is that what sets off the refrain about the bandits is a new malaise, something that makes my skin crawl every time I sweat my way through its magnificent and filthy alleys, every time an SUV forces me to flatten myself against the wall while I'm walking though the passageways of my native city. What is it? It's the impression that to the usual ills, the neglect, the degradation, the arrogance, the power in the hands of the few who treat it with total impunity as a personal domain and with a total lack of supervision—to all that there has been added a brazen postmodern patina. Bouncing power back and forth between the UDC and Forza Italia parties, it makes no difference what is really happening there, the evidence doesn't matter: whatever evidence there is can be covered up by a shrewd media blitz. The city has fallen into the snares of a television transformation, of a Mediaset blitz without equal in the rest of Europe. A mayor who should be ashamed of himself for the abysmal level of his own competence and for his total ignorance regarding the problems of the city, is instead worried about covering his ass after entrusting the image of Palermo to a team of experts, where image is understood to be the empty shadowy representation of a grandiloquence that says in big letters, "Palermo is cool," written as part of an overpriced campaign entrusted to Publicis shortly before the recent elections. This same first citizen, confronted with the tragedy of twenty-nine children of evicted families placed in the care of a community that has cut the funds for assistance to the homeless, children who with their families had occupied City Hall in order to draw the city's attention to the gravity of the problem, made himself scarce, refusing the make provisions for them and continuing to reiterate in public that with Wim Wenders filming *Palermo Shooting*, the city was now, as never before, at its maximum splendor. And a few weeks after, news came of another building collapse in the historic center, which buried a workman from a company called in at the last minute for "extraordinary maintenance." One has only to walk around a little in the center to be aware that the pollution is unbearable (the limit of the law is surpassed in double measure almost every day), that the garbage accumulates, that carjacking knows no limits, and that the degradation of the buildings is in direct proportion to the absence of regular maintenance, while the traffic is being managed by private companies who enrich themselves by removing an extraneous automobile from time to time.

The city is exhausted, sad; commercial dealings are weari-
some everywhere, unless it's laundering money for the mafia or
done by the "privileged" who can take advantage of mysterious
community loan opportunities. On the whole, it is a city that
has inexorably moved backwards in the last ten years; where the
quality of life and the condition of the environment are comparable only to the urban zone of Tamil Nadu or of the most disad-
vantaged Maghreb. The image, however, is saved. This ingen-
ious invention has been whacked into shape by the corporate
"media," who at the first victory of Forza Italia in the Council and
in the Region have taken possession of the city. Under the guid-
ance of a man of undoubted organizational skills, who emerged
from Mediaset and from *Paperissima* (and is today president of
the Triennale), and a newly minted creation, touted as "Grand
Events," the city has been reinvented, starting with popular cere-
monials. Under the management of Grand Events, the Feast of
Santa Rosalia has been expropriated from the crowd for whom
it has always been a fundamental date identifying the city, and
which has now been completely turned into a media event:
the Feast has become an event to be viewed on the screen, the
people of Palermo have to be content with a television image,
and it is of little importance that they are really right there in the
city. Through this highly original enterprise a whole strategy has
been coined, including the invention of a summer festival that
takes place among the ruins of the Kalsa, a festival celebrating
the "fascination of ruins," which takes something that in reality is degraded and wrecked so that all of a sudden it becomes
"picturesque." In short, over ten years of activity Grand Events
and all its creative team have taught the city not to see itself for
what it is, a place full of the unemployed, the homeless, with a
historic center without hope of restoration, an unproductive
city rife with extortion and corruption, but to see it instead as a
"very evocative," "very folkloric" location. The poor have been
scripted cheaply or for nothing into the poverty scenario. An
area of desperation and drug traffic such as the big Magione gash

has become the place of media-ized populism, where little kids hobnob with pushers and a bunch of scruffy types, and social centers play for free on improvised stages, while the powers-that-be of the city glorify themselves over the whole thing. In short, the late-lamented Baudrillard would say that it is brilliant, that right here in the shameful and Mafioso Italian subtopia, they are undertaking dress rehearsals for transforming reality to pure imagination—no matter that the rats are biting you or that the house is falling down around you. From this point of view the city has the most modern political class in the world, a class so inconsistent that now everyone identifies the mayor with the cartoon that portrayed him in the local pages of *La Repubblica* as a tennis racket backed by an invisible nonentity who speaks. One need only see how this man feared for his own seat at the UDC Convention during the last electoral campaign. Cuffaro made it quite clear to him, in front of everyone, that he is merely a puppet in the hands of the UDC and that his membership in Forza Italia is not enough to keep him afloat.

Since then, however, everyone has become more worked-up. The city is in the hands of the usual few, but they have managed to pry benevolent cooperation from those on the left who are disposed to sell themselves for a few good appointments. The system is efficient. Grand Events heaps strange inducements such as laughably low rents or special contracts on characters with a low cultural profile and who are amenable to making great compromises. Locations restored with public funds—theatres, cultural centers, sixteenth-century palaces—are placed under the management of these wheeler-dealers who then produce consensus by scattering a few appointments right and left. Thus everyone is happy and keeps quiet. So-called artistic directors publicize their offerings, which anywhere else would lead one to ask: but who is this person, what is his background? Palermo in the meantime becomes so pitiful with regards to theatrical productions—there still are some, but they are curtailed so as to concentrate all the power into the hands of the few—and so could not even participate in the competition to host the Italia Theatre Festival because of "lack of structure." Meanwhile, however, Grand Events boldly supports the hotshots who bring in design, new architecture, and second-hand glamour from Milan and a rehash of minor displays from the Triennale. With a remarkable turnover of money and profits, without open bids, public places are operated with private logic, in a city that gives thanks because at least someone is doing something, at least they don't have that sin of omission. Even I'm in line to say thanks, too. Without all this, without these contracts and debatable subconcessions, there would be even less; one accepts the fact that the city is agonizing, that a good number of the artists, the authors, the intellectuals, the musicians are constrained either to work elsewhere or simply to fall into line. My city has been like that forever. Monopoly becomes the norm: if you don't toe the line, you become marginalized; there is one bone and to gnaw on it for a morsel, it's worth the bother of standing in line behind the mastiffs. But I am doubtful whether between the system of extortion and this there is very much difference. But let's take careful note, because it's not like that. I made a mistake. This second system is extremely refined, it knows that things are what they seem to be, not what they are; and don't be surprised that at the end of it all even its victims are convinced: of course, "Palermo is cool," no doubt about it at all, it's the envy of everybody.

Milan–Bangalore Still Cool

After having written this piece on how things were going in Palermo, which was destined to appear in *Il Manifesto*, I noted that my overview had taught me something, but it was a bit blurry as far as local circumstances. I became aware of this reading an essay by Gayatri Chakravorty Spivak, "Bangalore, Megacity, 1997: Testing Theory in Cities."[2] Spivak is the most interesting of the postcolonial critics, a fine analyst of the ways globalization is manifesting itself in the suburbs of the world—from which she herself comes, having been born in Kolkata—and of how it has progressed, executing strange convolutions, apparently bizarre inversions, and above all how it is in the suburbs that one often tracks down situations of hypermodernity. Spivak explains how Bangalore, in Tamil Nadu, has become the city where the leading software companies of the world have transferred their bases. It is spoken of as the Silicon Valley of India; she talks however about "electronic capitalism." The new location of the installations is unimportant, but not the availability of low-cost qualified manpower: in short, the electronic engineers of Bangalore cost one-tenth of those in San Jose, California. The virtuality of the localization is offset by the frantic activities of a little class of jetlagged Indian managers created from the new distribution of financing and resources. Bangalore—and nowadays Hyderabad as well—has not however enjoyed an amelioration of its own real-life conditions. The cities bound up in this phenomenon have firstly lost the qualities that made them attractive in the eyes of the investors: they were small, unpolluted, they had a fresh climate from the high plains. But now that traffic has increased out of hand, they are overcrowded, and poverty has become more visible than before, since the boom of the Indian Silicon Valley has drawn enormous masses from the country. These are conditions common to many places in the suburbs of the world. The dislocation of productive activity creates pockets of wealth, which is immediately moved elsewhere from the local financial markets. The "trickle-down" effect is minimal, but it is enough to tempt new poor people who have abandoned the country to gamble on life in the city. The same thing happens too in the call-centers, but in this case we are dealing with a different dimension, with highly qualified people who are inducted into a productive bubble because they are offering themselves at a low cost.

Well, I rethought Palermo with regard to Bangalore. Palermo represents the suburbs of an Operetta Empire, Italy. Unlike Bangalore, we do not produce software technology here, but we do produce images, "symbolic capital," Bourdieu would have said, a virtual society of entertainment that turns

the entire city into a sideshow. It isn't even a question of tourism Barcelona-style. Here images of an "exotically impoverished"
city are constructed and sold, an Italian exoticism in the style of
Ciprì and Maresco, a little bit desperate, made up of palaces in
ruin and social disintegration. This image attracts not tourism,
but public investments for culture, and it is not by chance that
Fininvest, Berlusconi's Mediaset, are to be found in the middle
of the experiment. Palermo becomes a sales opportunity; as the
flyer says touting "Kals'art," the festival of art and entertainment
in the poorest and most abandoned part of the city: "the Arab
atmosphere of the alleys, where one still breathes in the oriental
world, and which finds here one of its most ancient manifesta-
tions." Palermo has become the object of a virtual architectonic
construction, and if huge sums for culture are being handled
here by the person who today directs the Triennale, so what. It
is clearly a question of spreading the simple message: the real
city is not what you see, but is that of media, the television idea
of Palermo (or Naples) in place of its reality. The city becomes
dematerialized, no more nor less than has happened through
the "electronic capitalism" of Bangalore. It doesn't matter that
Palermo is falling down around itself, that every day living there
gets worse, because it is the illusion that becomes the marketing
objective. This and nothing else is what is happening in general
in all the cities today. When I was talking about Manhattan and
of the totally bidimensional manner in which the new architecture is being installed there—for example, the famous much
loved "Riviera" grills by Steven Holl—I was thinking of the same
thing. The new architecture is communications, media, and the
substantiation of the city must go and be blessed. Because this
project, if it is to happen, needs first of all to convince the inhabitants that the image-touting campaigns are more important
than services and the quality of life. The Publicis campaign for
Palermo cost about as much as a general environmental restoration of the historic center, but it has achieved its effect of
convincing the inhabitants that Palermo is cool, and woe to

those who speak ill of her. Saviano talked about the same affect in Naples, where alongside a mountain of garbage that no one dares to remove arise the symbols of the spirit of Naples, like the enormous shopping center in the shape of Vesuvius commissioned from Renzo Piano. The vocation of the architectural profession today is to dematerialize the city, to remove from it the daily flesh of its stones and its inhabitants and to transform it into liquid crystal. Milan is nothing less. Every time I go there I am astounded that faced with such a widespread diffusion of degraded living conditions, one can still accept the glossy monumentality of the giant posters of the big names in fashion. It is a city that proclaims that it is unable to do anything, that it cannot begin to think about an amelioration of the urban décor, or ordinary maintenance, or of making an investment thanks to which the subway might stop being the most squalid on the planet. But no, being the capital of the Operetta Empire, everything is delegated to the image—if it deprives the city of a park, as at Isola, the quick response is that it is for the benefit of the skyline, a somewhat outdated concept, but which "takes" because Milan is the first victim of its bidimensional varnishing. We are in an internal postcolonial condition; we have become colonialists: selling off our territory at a loss to the logic of a media-based abstraction with no relationship to real life, to how people live in a place, we have reduced it to a brand that superimposes itself, like a luminous sign, over the mountains of garbage and the neglect accumulating behind it. La Brianza and Milan itself are the forgotten remnant of an aborted industrial revolution that did not have the courage to challenge itself and be environmentally restored to health. It is not by chance, moreover, that this could happen in the homeland of Fiat. Mediaset has succeeded in ratcheting it up a notch. It went from closing the factory to selling out the territory as a pure potential of illusions. The city today is submerged under total Mediaset-ification: under the guise of "cultural activities, grand events," a voracious vacuum cleaner is transforming the missing services into images, along with the housing that is not being built, the parks that are being forgotten. Milan and Palermo and Naples are models perhaps even more advanced than Bangalore, because they represent the dissolution of the city as a physical entity and its replacement (in the midst of the city's death throes) by its sellable simulacrum. It is Italy that, as a place of image capitalism, has taken from the information revolution not the potential of connecting with the rest of the world, but the brutal reduction of reality to a media surrogate. Mike Davis would speak of the "evil paradises," and in reality Milan or Palermo or Naples are paradises only for those who don't ever take off those glasses that once upon a time they distributed at cinemas when they were showing 3-D movies.[3] And it doesn't matter that the stink of the garbage prevents their using their other senses.

But Spivak's article also talks about "radical architects" who in Kolkata as well as in Bangalore are fighting this tendency towards virtuality. Therefore the profession can still be credited with an uncomfortable, critical, and intellectual role. It is beautiful to hear it said, and it would be interesting for us too, the country of architects *par excellence*, if there were at least a tiny group capable of opposing the "chic" dissolution of the city.

NOTES

1.   Kevin Kelly, *New Rules for the New Economy: 10 Ways the Network Economy Is Changing Everything* (New York: Viking 1998), 76.
2.   Gayatri Chakravorty Spivak, *Other Cities* (Malden, MA: Blackwell, 2008)
3.   Mike Davis and Daniel Bertrand Monk, eds., *Evil Paradises: Dreamworlds of Neoliberalism* (New York: The New Press, 2007).

CHAPTER 7

The New Banks
of Happiness

Llevaba una ciudad dentro
Y la perdia sin combate
Y le perdieron

He carried a city within him.
He lost it.
And they defeated him.

—Rafael Alberti, *Concerning the Angels*
(Christopher Sawyer-Lauçanno, trans.)

ALLOW ME TO SAY AT THIS POINT THAT WE ALL STAND TO
gain from an architectural recession, including, alas, the architects. It is by now fairly clear that compromised as they are in their
attempt to participate in the festivities of Casino Capitalism, they
have long since lost the sense of a profession that could still prove
useful: a sense of public space, the intuition and vision required
to plan and explore the future with all its accompanying options,
without necessarily implementing it right away, the utopian ability
to conceptualize human coexistence as a dialectic between identity and place. Right now we've missed the boat, and for sure there
won't be another one for quite some time. The risk is that other
technocrats, far more powerful and better-prepared than these
so-called trapeze artists (the idea that a profession so bound up
with the earth could be transformed into a high-wire three-ring
circus act makes some of us very angry) may well take possession
of this domain. Architectural schools give us little cause for hope.
Every year Italy turns out thousands of new architects, diplomas in

hand, all of them determined to win the Grand Prix of the profession. The lust-driven models to which they subscribe are those that fall under the rubric of the unbridled freedom of the Genius, a hybrid of tsarist power and academic influence-mongering.

Places such as the IUAV, the Venice University Institute of Architecture, which could theoretically play a leadership role in reforming the profession, are rooted in corporate interests, either incapable of grasping the overarching problems of urban administrations, or else are woefully committed to an obsolete concept of city planning. Architecture students are not trained in the way cities really work, the kind of things taught in any Public Health course in the United States. Faced by an international demand for experts in urban habitat, Venice—in lockstep with the majority of departments of architecture in Italy, churns out a steady stream of pampered prodigies who have no intuitive understanding of the setting in which they are going to work. None of the concepts and research instruments developed over the past century by the human sciences has made the slightest dent in the conviction that architecture is done "in house," that the drawing-board is the best teacher. As a result, the patrimony of fieldwork, such a crucial requirement in a profession where understanding context is essential, is completely ignored by everyone: the students are not equipped with the tools to observe, analyze, and decipher the social impact of the built projects they design. The core principle of environmental sustainability has just won acceptance, adopted as if it were a mere technical detail, a question of hygienic infrastructure without an overarching vision of the relationship between resources and territory. This old convention is not about the die out. And so we produce frustrated people who continue to perpetuate self-indulgent practices for a city that actually demands a strong attitude of direct confrontation, a capacity for a one-on-one relationship.

What to do? Ignore this state of pathetic decline, confident that either way the cities will continue to go about their own business? Today the real situation threatening to strangle city life is not the collision between the formalism of the architects and the practicalities of living: formalism is a façade that covers the most efficacious operations, those of order and control on the one side, and on the other, those that integrally transform cities into virtual real estate arenas.

The police and their connection with security have become the watchword of the new middle classes, a watchword that doesn't do much for them, but eliminates all the unpredictable and multi-functional things that happen in a city. Today there are in-depth studies into the counterproductive effect of police management of the city, studies that confirm that a democracy cannot allow itself to entrust its urban management to vigilantes, whether public or private. And this version of police rule is even more aberrant because it is based on the idea that citizens' mobility functions like vehicular traffic. The automobile is what has destroyed the rights of the street, the right to use public space as the space for the creation of urban culture. The automobile has become the most ruthless police system that could ever have been invented, transforming any movement of the citizenry into a constant state of alarm. In this sense the car accomplishes a biopolice inter-vention, because it replaces the body of the citizen with a metal wrapper, and from the beginning makes it into an object to be crushed, as Ballard so wittily demonstrated in *Crash*, and as does the American artist Liz Cohen, who reinvents her figure—body-building—in front of parades of cars—while she reinvents the perfect car—body parts—a hybrid of a Trabant and an El Camino. Kenneth Frampton says that one can never denounce with suffi-cient force the destructive consequences the automobile has had on the city forever, indeed demolishing it, turning it into merely a secondary background for moving itself and parking itself.

Is there any hope? Yes, there is, because life resists the most ferocious repressions, and even after being evicted, relocation ends up restoring the fabric of consciousness and symbolic inher-itance, conscious or subconscious, which enables one to live in a place, with a place. This "local frame of mind," like a living language, can be humiliated, prohibited, but it remains difficult to eradicate from it its intrinsic skills. Architecture decided at a certain point to have nothing more to do with that, after the fall of the Wall and the ideologies, to leave the local frame of mind to itself, so that today it is no longer able to interpret it.

Instead, we have to lend a new ear to the possibilities of urban space, which are many, myriad.

In a magnificent book on the "History of Collective Joy," entitled *Dancing in the Streets,* Barbara Ehrenreich has reconstructed the history of group ecstasy, from the Dionysian festivals to the dances inside churches up to the invention of Carnival, to its Puritan and military repression, to the epidemic of melancholia that ensued, to Fascist regimentation, to the rock revolution, to sport and to today's rebirth of the sense of public space as a possible place of collective happiness, to an ecstasy of dance and politics that from time to time reemerges in the counterculture, in the Orange Revolution in Ukraine, in rap and hip-hop, in "pasear y ramblear." Barbara Ehrenreich does not say that the revival of joy in the streets is impossible but rather that the festival is something of which that *possibility* might leap into the eye of a foreign beholder of our cities. Listen:

> Nineteenth-century Protestant Reformers sometimes sought to shame European carnival-goers by imagining the reaction of a converted "Hottentot" to such unseemly goings-on. The converted savage would, in these fanciful accounts, be disgusted to find supposedly civilized Christians dancing, masking, and cavorting in public exactly like his unconverted brethren at home. But the more interesting case would be that of an *un*converted "savage" plopped down in the modern urban world—say, an eighteenth-century indigenous Australian, Plains Indian, or resident of New Guinea—transported into midtown Manhattan, just as the lunch-hour crowds are hitting the street.

He will necessarily be dumbfounded by flashing lights, automobiles, and the near-complete replacement of trees and grass by a built environment. But leaving aside the technological future-shock, with all its comic possibilities, what will amaze him most is the size of the crowd he finds himself in: as many people, within a block or so, as he has ever seen together in his life, and then only at the annual gatherings of his tribe, where several hundred people might come together at a time, for days of dancing, feasting, and other carnival-like activities.

In his experience, a crowd is the raw material for festivity, and a large crowd is the making of more intense and creative festivity than anything that can be generated in his own band of a few dozen people. For a moment, the prevalence of face paint on the New Yorkers and—from our "savage's" point of view—their universal "costuming" may fool him into thinking he has emerged into a similar kind of festivity, but the facial expressions of the people around him will immediately belie this supposition. The faces are closed, unsmiling, intent on unknown missions, wary of eye contact. Whatever these people are doing, they are not celebrating. And this will be the biggest shock to him: their refusal, or inability, to put this abundant convergence of humanity to use for some kind of celebration.[1]

Barbara Ehrenreich naturally leads us to rediscover that in some way cities are born to give a crowd an opportunity to find something to celebrate. Isn't this perhaps a remnant of collective happiness, something that hardly happens to us when we go shopping? "Fashion makes us happy for half an hour at most," as I have affirmed elsewhere. Isn't this what we are still looking for when we break out of our private cells to surge in the streets, to reconquer them as we risk our lives to the repressive power of the automobiles? One could interpret the public use of the city as the daily story of a collective resistance to the disembodiment of the city itself, to the humiliation of its body by a band of madmen from Casino Capitalism. And in order to delude itself, this same Casino Capitalism needs to make-believe that there is a festival, and it's being celebrated somewhere, in the shops, in the shopping malls, in front of shop windows. The problem is that we let them cheat us by their transformation of the crowd's desire for dance and urban ecstasy, into marketing and publicity, of which branding is only a version for simpletons. Cities produce much more than trends, than brands and logos, they are the places where it is still possible to play the collective game of identities, where it is possible to go out and become part of the scene, to see and be seen, to touch and be touched. Ehrenreich enables us to regain the vividness of desire for space and the city, a vividness that is not negated by the simple observation that the "lonely crowd" is by now only prey for occult persuaders. The city resists, as Spivak also says, in the waxing and waning of its popula-tion, in their self-recognition in the spirit of place, in their simple wish to use it for their own reasons of joy and sorrow, a kind of accomplishment that thwarts all the aims and deeds of dispossession by the fatal world of architecture and branding.

The city is a place of the circulation of significant material, flowing just as a river flows between banks of happiness. Like the river of which Guimarães Rosa speaks, the city is the inven-tion of a movement that is able to watch itself, to stop and watch itself flowing, and to start going again in order to feel itself part of a flow. For such a city it is worthwhile to invent a new exper-tise, an attentive, lively, profound discipline, with on-the-spot investigators, connoisseurs of life-styles and living styles, stable visionaries, scientists of human nature who do not, like every stupid little provincial artist, allow themselves to feel superior to it, all of them wanting to learn the dance so they can defend it between the new banks of happiness.

NOTES

1.   Barbara Ehrenreich, *Dancing in the Streets. A History of Collective Joy* (New York: Metropolitan Books, 2007), 247 et seq.

Author: Franco La Cecla

Born in Palermo in 1950, Franco La Cecla is a renowned anthro-pologist and architect. He has taught anthropology in many European cities such as Palermo, Venice, Verona, Paris, and Barcelona. He has worked as a consultant for the Renzo Piano Building Workshop and for Barcelona Regional. In 2005 he founded the Architecture Social Impact Assessment, ASIA, an agency that evaluates the social impact of architectural and city planning projects. In addition he has created several documen-taries, one of which, *In altro mare* (In another sea) won the Best Coastal Culture Film award at the 2010 San Francisco Ocean Film Festival. Franco La Cecla is currently in production with RAI television on a series based on *Against Architecture*.

Translator: Mairin O'Mahony

Mairin O'Mahony was born in London, where she worked as an editor for thirteen years before moving to San Francisco. Her experience includes a wide variety of copywriting on subjects ranging from agriculture to finance to travel. She is a passionate Italophile, dividing her time between San Francisco and Italy.

Credo of The Green Arcade

The Green Arcade, a curated bookstore, specializes in sustainability, from the built environment to the natural world. The Green Arcade is a meeting place for rebels, flaneurs, farmers, and architects: those who build, inhabit, and add something valuable to the world.

The Green Arcade

1680 Market Street

San Francisco, CA 94102–5949

www.thegreenarcade.com

ABOUT PM PRESS

PM Press was founded at the end of 2007 by a small collection of folks with decades of publishing, media, and organizing experience. PM Press co-conspirators have published and distributed hundreds of books, pamphlets, CDs, and DVDs. Members of PM have founded enduring book fairs, spearheaded victorious tenant organizing campaigns, and worked closely with bookstores, academic conferences, and even rock bands to deliver political and challenging ideas to all walks of life. We're old enough to know what we're doing and young enough to know what's at stake.

We seek to create radical and stimulating fiction and non-fiction books, pamphlets, t-shirts, visual and audio materials to entertain, educate and inspire you. We aim to distribute these through every available channel with every available technology — whether that means you are seeing anarchist classics at our bookfair stalls; reading our latest vegan cookbook at the café; downloading geeky fiction e-books; or digging new music and timely videos from our website.

PM Press is always on the lookout for talented and skilled volunteers, artists, activists and writers to work with. If you have a great idea for a project or can contribute in some way, please get in touch.

PM Press
PO Box 23912
Oakland, CA 94623
www.pmpress.org

FRIENDS OF PM PRESS

These are indisputably momentous times—the financial system is melting down globally and the Empire is stumbling. Now more than ever there is a vital need for radical ideas.

In the four years since its founding—and on a mere shoestring—PM Press has risen to the formidable challenge of publishing and distributing knowledge and entertainment for the struggles ahead. With over 175 releases to date, we have published an impressive and stimulating array of literature, art, music, politics, and culture. Using every available medium, we've succeeded in connecting those hungry for ideas and information to those putting them into practice.

Friends of PM allows you to directly help impact, amplify, and revitalize the discourse and actions of radical writers, filmmakers, and artists. It provides us with a stable foundation from which we can build upon our early successes and provides a much-needed subsidy for the materials that can't necessarily pay their own way. You can help make that happen—and receive every new title automatically delivered to your door once a month—by joining as a Friend of PM Press. And, we'll throw in a free T-shirt when you sign up.

Here are your options:

- **$25 a month** Get all books and pamphlets plus 50% discount on all webstore purchases

- **$40 a month** Get all PM Press releases (including CDs and DVDs) plus 50% discount on all webstore purchases

- **$100 a month** Superstar—Everything plus PM merchandise, free downloads, and 50% discount on all webstore purchases

For those who can't afford $25 or more a month, we're introducing **Sustainer Rates** at $15, $10 and $5. Sustainers get a free PM Press T-shirt and a 50% discount on all purchases from our website.

Your Visa or Mastercard will be billed once a month, until you tell us to stop. Or until our efforts succeed in bringing the revolution around. Or the financial meltdown of Capital makes plastic redundant. Whichever comes first.

with PM Press
Low Bite
Sin Soracco

ISBN: 978-1-60486-226-3
$14.95   144 pages

Low Bite Sin Soracco's prison novel about survival, dignity, friendship and insubordination. The view from inside a women's prison isn't a pretty one, and Morgan, the narrator, knows that as well as anyone. White, female, 26, convicted of night time breaking and entering with force, she works in the prison law library, giving legal counsel of more-or-mostly-less usefulness to other convicts. More useful is the hootch stash she keeps behind the law books.

And she has plenty of enemies—like Johnson, the lesbian-hating warden, and Alex, the "pretty little dude" lawyer who doesn't like her free legal advice. Then there's Rosalie and Birdeye—serious rustlers whose loyalty lasts about as long as their cigarettes hold out. And then there's China: Latina, female, 22, holding US citizenship through marriage, convicted of conspiracy to commit murder—a dangerous woman who is safer in prison than she is on the streets. They're all trying to get through without getting caught or going straight, but there's just one catch—a bloodstained bank account that everybody wants, including some players on the outside. *Low Bite*: an underground classic reprinted at last and the first title in the new imprint from The Green Arcade.

"Vicious, funny, cunning, ruthless, explicit… a tough original look at inside loves and larcenies."
— Kirkus Reviews

"Where else can you find the grittiness of girls-behind-bars mixed with intelligence, brilliant prose, and emotional ferocity? Sin Soracco sets the standard for prison writing. Hardboiled and with brains!"
— Peter Maravelis, editor *San Francisco Noir* 1 and 2

"Tells a gripping story concerning a group of women in a California prison: their crimes, their relationships, their hopes and dreams."
— Publisher's Weekly

with PM Press
A Moment of Doubt
Jim Nisbet

ISBN: 978-1-60486-307-9
$13.95   144 pages

A Moment of Doubt is at turns hilarious,
thrilling and obscene. Jim Nisbet's novella
is ripped from the zeitgeist of the 80s, and
set in a sex-drenched San Francisco, where
the computer becomes the protagonist's
co-conspirator and both writer and machine
seem to threaten the written word itself. The City as whore provides
a backdrop oozing with drugs, poets and danger. Nisbet has written
a mad-cap meditation on the angst of a writer caught in a world
where the rent is due, new technology offers up illicit ways to
produce the latest bestseller, and the detective and other characters
of the imagination might just sidle up to the bar and buy you a drink
in real life. The world of *A Moment of Doubt* is the world of phone sex,
bars and bordellos, AIDS and the lure of hacking. Coming up against
the rules of the game—the detective genre itself, has never been
such a nasty and gender defying challenge.

Plus: An interview with Jim Nisbet, who is "Still too little read in the
United States, it's a joy for us that Nisbet has been recognized here..."
Regards: Le Mouvement des Idées

*"He is as weird as the world. And for some readers, that's a quality to
cherish. It's as if Nisbet inhabited and wrote from a world right next to
ours, only weirder."*
— Rick Kleffel, bookotron.com

*"Missing any book by Nisbet should be considered a crime in all 50
states and maybe against humanity."*
— Bill Ott, *Booklist*

*"With Nisbet, you know you can expect anything and you're never
disappointed."*
— Le Figaro

*"Jim Nisbet is a poet... [who] resembles no other crime fiction writer.
He mixes the irony of Dantesque situations with lyric narration, and
achieves a luxuriant cocktail that truly leaves the reader breathless."*
— Drood's Review of Mysteries

West of Eden: Communes and Utopia in Northern California

Edited by Iain Boal, Janferie Stone,
Michael Watts, and Cal Winslow

ISBN: 978-1-60486-427-4
$24.95   304 pages

In the shadow of the Vietnam war, a
significant part of an entire generation
refused their assigned roles in the American
century. Some took their revolutionary politics to the streets, others
decided simply to turn away, seeking to build another world together,
outside the state and the market. *West of Eden* charts the remarkable
flowering of communalism in the '60s and '70s, fueled by a radical
rejection of the Cold War corporate deal, utopian visions of a
peaceful green planet, the new technologies of sound and light, and
the ancient arts of ecstatic release. Using memoir and flashbacks,
oral history and archival sources, *West of Eden* explores the deep
historical roots and the enduring, though often disavowed, legacies
of the extraordinary pulse of radical energies that generated forms
of collective life beyond the nuclear family and the world of private
consumption. *West of Eden* is not only a necessary act of reclamation,
but is also intended as an offering to the coming generation who
will find here, in the rubble of the twentieth century, a past they can
use—indeed one they will need—in the passage from the privations
of commodity capitalism to an ample life in common.

*"As a gray army of undertakers gather in Sacramento to bury California's
great dreams of equality and justice, this wonderful book, with its faith
in the continuity of our state's radical-communitarian ethic, replants the
seedbeds of defiant imagination and hopeful resistance."*
— Mike Davis, author of *City of Quartz* and *Magical Urbanism*

"Utopias—we can't live without them, nor within them, for long. In
West of Eden *we see California, an earthly utopia, and the Sixties, a
utopian moment, in full flower. Brave souls creating a heavenly host
of communal spaces on the edge of America, hoping to break free of
a world of capital, sexism, oligarchy, race. An amazing place and time
that, for all its failures, changed the world—and which finally gets its
due in this marvelous collection."*
— Richard Walker, UC Berkeley, author of *The Country in The City*

The Paul Goodman Reader
Edited by Taylor Stoehr
ISBN: 978-1-60486-058-0
$28.95   500 pages

A one-man think-tank for the New Left, Paul Goodman wrote over thirty books, most of them before his decade of fame as a social critic in the Sixties. A Paul Goodman Reader that does him justice must be a compendious volume, with excerpts not only from best-sellers like *Growing Up Absurd*, but also from his landmark books on education, community planning, anarchism, psychotherapy, language theory, and poetics. Samples as well from *The Empire City*, a comic novel reviewers compared to *Don Quixote*, prize-winning short stories, and scores of poems that led America's most respected poetry reviewer, Hayden Carruth, to exclaim, "Not one dull page. It's almost unbelievable."

Goodman called himself as an old-fashioned man of letters, which meant that all these various disciplines and occasions added up to a single abiding concern for the human plight in perilous times, and for human promise and achieved grandeur, love and hope.

"It was that voice of his that seduced me—that direct, cranky, egotistical, generous American voice... Paul Goodman's voice touched everything he wrote about with intensity, interest, and his own terribly appealing sureness and awkwardness... It was his voice, that is to say, his intelligence and the poetry of his intelligence incarnated, which kept me a loyal and passionate fan."
— Susan Sontag, novelist and public intellectual

"Goodman, like all real novelists, is, at bottom, a moralist. What really interests him are the various ways in which human beings living in a modern metropolis gain, keep or lose their integrity and sense of selfhood."
— W. H. Auden, poet

"Any page by Paul Goodman will give you not only originality and brilliance but wisdom, that is, something to think about. He is our peculiar, urban, twentieth-century Thoreau, the quintessential American mind of our time."
— Hayden Carruth, poet and essayist

London Peculiar and Other Nonfiction

Michael Moorcock. Edited by Allan Kausch with an introduction by Iain Sinclair

ISBN: 978-1-60486-490-8
$23.95   408 pages

Voted by the London *Times* as one of the best writers since 1945, Michael Moorcock was shortlisted for the Whitbread Prize and won the Guardian Fiction Prize. He has won almost all the major Science Fiction, Fantasy, and lifetime achievement awards including the "Howie," the Prix Utopiales and the Stoker. Best known for his rule-breaking SF and Fantasy, including the classic Elric and Hawkmoon series, he is also the author of several graphic novels. Now, in *London Peculiar and Other Nonfiction*, Michael Moorcock personally selects the best of his published, unpublished, and uncensored essays, articles, reviews, and opinions covering a wide range of subjects: books, films, politics, reminiscences of old friends, and attacks on new foes. Drawn from over fifty years of writing, the pieces in *London Peculiar and Other Nonfiction* showcase Moorcock at his acerbic best.

"Moorcock's reviews and critical essays seem to me exemplary. They are never routine, never obligatory, never tired. They seem to me to be models of what a creative writer should do when producing critical prose. His writing here is always a conversation, never a monologue… we feel lucky to be listening in."
—Alan Wall, writer, poet, and Professor of Writing and Literature at the University of Chester, UK.

"London Peculiar is the first full sampling of Moorcock's most important and imperishable musings on subjects both vast and various: movies and music, science and politics, the old days at New Worlds, from Philip K. Dick to R. Crumb, classics from Huxley to Pynchon, and tasty tidbits from the Tea Party to Texas barbecue. Gleaned from a full half century of opinion and outcry, London Peculiar is the work of a man of letters in the grand tradition of Orwell and Dr. Johnson. It's Old School and it's all you need to know about Tomorrow."
— Terry Bisson, Hugo and Nebula award-winning novelist

Demanding the Impossible: A History of Anarchism

Peter Marshall

ISBN: 978-1-60486-064-1
$28.95   840 pages

Navigating the broad 'river of anarchy',
from Taoism to Situationism, from Ranters
to Punk rockers, from individualists to
communists, from anarcho-syndicalists to
anarcha-feminists, Demanding the Impossible
is an authoritative and lively study of a widely misunderstood
subject. It explores the key anarchist concepts of society and the
state, freedom and equality, authority and power and investigates
the successes and failure of the anarchist movements throughout
the world. While remaining sympathetic to anarchism, it presents a
balanced and critical account. It covers not only the classic anarchist
thinkers, such as Godwin, Proudhon, Bakunin, Kropotkin, Reclus and
Emma Goldman, but also other libertarian figures, such as Nietzsche,
Camus, Gandhi, Foucault and Chomsky. No other book on anarchism
covers so much so incisively.

In this updated edition, a new epilogue examines the most recent
developments, including 'post-anarchism' and 'anarcho-primitivism'
as well as the anarchist contribution to the peace, green and 'Global
Justice' movements.

Demanding the Impossible is essential reading for anyone wishing to
understand what anarchists stand for and what they have achieved.
It will also appeal to those who want to discover how anarchism
offers an inspiring and original body of ideas and practices which is
more relevant than ever in the twenty-first century.

"Demanding the Impossible *is the book I always recommend when
asked—as I often am—for something on the history and ideas of
anarchism.*"
— Noam Chomsky

"*Attractively written and fully referenced… bound to be the standard
history.*"
— Colin Ward, *Times Educational Supplement*

Also from ■SPECTRE▶ from PM Press

Capital and Its Discontents: Conversations with Radical Thinkers in a Time of Tumult

Sasha Lilley

ISBN: 978-1-60486-334-5
$20.00   320 pages

Capitalism is stumbling, empire is faltering, and the planet is thawing. Yet many people are still grasping to understand these multiple crises and to find a way forward to a just future. Into the breach come the essential insights of *Capital and Its Discontents*, which cut through the gristle to get to the heart of the matter about the nature of capitalism and imperialism, capitalism's vulnerabilities at this conjuncture—and what can we do to hasten its demise. Through a series of incisive conversations with some of the most eminent thinkers and political economists on the Left—including David Harvey, Ellen Meiksins Wood, Mike Davis, Leo Panitch, Tariq Ali, and Noam Chomsky—*Capital and Its Discontents* illuminates the dynamic contradictions undergirding capitalism and the potential for its dethroning. At a moment when capitalism as a system is more reviled than ever, here is an indispensable toolbox of ideas for action by some of the most brilliant thinkers of our times.

"*These conversations illuminate the current world situation in ways that are very useful for those hoping to orient themselves and find a way forward to effective individual and collective action. Highly recommended.*"
—Kim Stanley Robinson, *New York Times* bestselling author of the *Mars Trilogy* and *The Years of Rice and Salt*

"*In this fine set of interviews, an A-list of radical political economists demonstrate why their skills are indispensable to understanding today's multiple economic and ecological crises.*"
—Raj Patel, author of *Stuffed and Starved* and *The Value of Nothing*

"*This is an extremely important book. It is the most detailed, comprehensive, and best study yet published on the most recent capitalist crisis and its discontents. Sasha Lilley sets each interview in its context, writing with style, scholarship, and wit about ideas and philosophies.*"
—Andrej Grubačić, radical sociologist and social critic, co-author of *Wobblies and Zapatistas*

William Morris: Romantic to Revolutionary

E.P. Thompson
with a foreword by Peter Linebaugh

ISBN: 978-1-60486-243-0
$32.95   880 pages

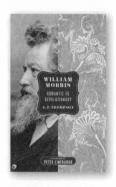

William Morris—the great 19th century craftsman, architect, designer, poet, and writer—remains a monumental figure whose influence resonates powerfully today. As an intellectual (and author of the seminal utopian *News From Nowhere*), his concern with artistic and human values led him to cross what he called the 'river of fire' and become a committed socialist—committed not to some theoretical formula but to the day by day struggle of working women and men in Britain and to the evolution of his ideas about art, about work and about how life should be lived.

Many of his ideas accorded none too well with the reforming tendencies dominant in the labour movement, nor with those of 'orthodox' Marxism, which has looked elsewhere for inspiration. Both sides have been inclined to venerate Morris rather than to pay attention to what he said.

Originally written less than a decade before his groundbreaking *The Making of the English Working Class*, E.P. Thompson brought to this biography his now trademark historical mastery, passion, wit, and essential sympathy. It remains unsurpassed as the definitive work on this remarkable figure, by the major British historian of the 20th century.

"Two impressive figures, William Morris as subject and E. P. Thompson as author, are conjoined in this immense biographical-historical-critical study, and both of them have gained in stature since the first edition of the book was published… The book that was ignored in 1955 has meanwhile become something of an underground classic—almost impossible to locate in second-hand bookstores, pored over in libraries, required reading for anyone interested in Morris and, increasingly, for anyone interested in one of the most important of contemporary British historians… Thompson has the distinguishing characteristic of a great

Vida

Marge Piercy

ISBN: 978-1-60486-487-8
$20.00   416 pages

Originally published in 1979, *Vida* is Marge
Piercy's classic bookend to the Sixties.
Vida is full of the pleasures and pains, the
experiments, disasters, and victories of an
extraordinary band of people. At the center
of the novel stands Vida Asch. She has
lived underground for almost a decade. Back in the '60s she was
a political star of the exuberant antiwar movement—a red-haired
beauty photographed for the pages of *Life* magazine—charismatic,
passionate, and totally sure she would prevail. Now, a decade later,
Vida is on the run, her star-quality replaced by stubborn courage.
She comes briefly to rest in a safe house on Cape Cod. To her
surprise and annoyance, she finds another person in the house, a
fugitive, Joel, ten years younger than she, a kid who dropped into the
underground out of the army. As they spend the next days together,
Vida finds herself warming toward a man for the first time in years,
knowing all too well the dangers.

As counterpoint to the underground '70s, Marge Piercy tells the
extraordinary tale of the optimistic '60s, the thousands of people
who were members of SAW (Students Against the War) and of
the handful who formed a fierce group called the Little Red Wagon.
Piercy's characters make vivid and comprehensible the desperation,
the courage, and the blind rage of a time when "action" could appear
to some to be a more rational choice than the vote.

A new introduction by Marge Piercy situates the book, and the
author, in the times from which they emerged.

*"Real people inhabit its pages and real suspense carries the story along…
'Vida' of course means life and she personifies it."*
— *Chicago Tribune*

*"A fully controlled, tightly structured dramatic narrative of such artful
intensity that it leads the reader on at almost every page."*
— *New York Times Book Review*

The Wild Girls

Ursula K. Le Guin

ISBN: 978-1-60486-403-8
$12.00   112 pages

Ursula K. Le Guin is the one modern science fiction author who truly needs no introduction. In the forty years since *The Left Hand of Darkness*, her works have changed not only the face but the tone and the agenda of SF, introducing themes of gender, race, socialism and anarchism, all the while thrilling readers with trips to strange (and strangely familiar) new worlds. She is our exemplar of what fantastic literature can and should be about.

Her Nebula winner *The Wild Girls*, newly revised and presented here in book form for the first time, tells of two captive "dirt children" in a society of sword and silk, whose determination to enter "that possible even when unattainable space in which there is room for justice" leads to a violent and loving end.

Plus: Le Guin's scandalous and scorching Harper's essay, 'Staying Awake While We Read', (also collected here for the first time) which demolishes the pretensions of corporate publishing and the basic assumptions of capitalism as well. And of course our Outspoken Interview which promises to reveal the hidden dimensions of America's best-known SF author. And delivers.

"Idiosyncratic and convincing, Le Guin's characters have a long afterlife."
— *Publishers Weekly*

"Her worlds are haunting psychological visions molded with firm artistry."
— *The Library Journal*

"If you want excess and risk and intelligence, try Le Guin."
— *The San Francisco Chronicle*

"Her characters are complex and haunting, and her writing is remarkable for its sinewy grace."
— *Time*